HISTORY LIVES
VOLUME THREE

COURAGE

AND

CONVICTION

CHRONICLES OF

THE REFORMATION CHURCH

HISTORY LIVES
VOLUME THREE

COURAGE
AND CONVICTION

CHRONICLES OF
THE REFORMATION CHURCH

MINDY AND
BRANDON WITHROW

CHRISTIAN FOCUS

For Sarah,
Connor,
and Nicole

May you be pilgrims of this world
and citizens of heaven.

CONTENTS

REFORMATION CHURCH TIMELINE
1500-1700

1492	Christopher Columbus reaches North America
1500	Pencil invented in England
1503	Leonardo da Vinci completes *Mona Lisa*
1508	Henry VIII ascends to English throne
1511	Desiderius Erasmus publishes *In Praise of Folly*
1512	Michelangelo completes Sistine Chapel
1517	Martin Luther posts "95 Theses" in Wittenberg
1519	Ulrich Zwingli preaches reformation in Switzerland
1521	Martin Luther excommunicated by Pope Leo X
1525	Peasants' War in Germany; Anabaptist movement begins
1526	William Tyndale publishes English New Testament
1527	Luther writes hymn "A Mighty Fortress is Our God"
1533	Thomas Cranmer becomes Archbishop of Canterbury
1534	Church of England separates from Rome; city of Münster taken by Anabaptists
1536	Menno Simons becomes Anabaptist leader in Holland; John Calvin publishes first edition of *Institutes of the Christian Religion*
1543	Nicolaus Copernicus publishes *On the Revolutions of Heavenly Bodies*
1545	Katherine Parr publishes *Prayers or Meditations*; Anne Askew burned at the stake; Council of Trent begins
1547	Henry VIII of England dies; Edward VI ascends throne
1552	*Book of Common Prayer* published
1553	Mary Tudor ascends English throne
1555	Nicholas Ridley and Hugh Latimer burned at the stake by Mary Tudor
1556	Thomas Cranmer burned at the stake by Mary Tudor

1558	Elizabeth I ascends English throne
1560	Jeanne d'Albret converts to Protestantism; French Calvinists first called Huguenots; John Knox publishes *First Book of Discipline*
1572	St. Bartholomew's Day Massacre
1596	Thermometer invented; Rene Descartes born
1598	Henry IV of France signs Edict of Nantes, ending French Wars of Religion
1601	William Shakespeare publishes *Hamlet*
1603	James VI of Scotland ascends English throne as James I of England and Scotland
1605	Telescope invented
1611	"King James Version," Bible translation authorized by James I of England, published
1619	Synod of Dort
1620	The Mayflower lands at Plymouth Rock
1634	Catholics found Maryland Colony
1647	Westminster Assembly ratifies *Westminster Confession of Faith*
1661	Louis XIV of France begins construction on Versailles
1663	John Eliot publishes Algonquian Bible, first Bible printed in America
1666	Great Fire of London
1675	King Philip's War begins in Massachusetts
1678	John Bunyan publishes *Pilgrim's Progress*
1685	Johann Sebastian Bach born
1689	Peter the Great becomes Tsar of Russia
1692	Salem witch trials execute twenty people
1700	Amish split from Swiss Brethren

WHAT WAS THE REFORMATION CHURCH?

THE WORD REFORMATION is a call for renewal or change. In the church, reformation is a call for renewal or change in Christian doctrine or practice. Since the beginning of the church, Christians have always found reasons for reform. When the church failed to meet the needs of the poor, for example, monks started hospitals and soup kitchens. When bishops abused their authority, theologians reminded them of Christ's humility. During the *Medieval* era, men like John Wyclif and John Hus began to question the pope's authority.

By the time of the *Renaissance*—a movement beginning in the fifteenth century that revived the study of history, literature, and languages—inventions like the printing press helped spread ideas more quickly. The word *reform* was on the lips of many, but they did not agree on what changes should be made or how to make them. Often, men and women who called for reform became unpopular with church leaders, who saw them as a threat to the established church. These *reformers* laid the foundation for a period of history from about 1500 to 1700 we call the *Reformation*.

THE BEGINNING OF THE REFORMATION

The first reformer of this new era was Desiderius Erasmus of Rotterdam. Erasmus was a teacher and a leader of the Renaissance. Many leaders of the Reformation were educated in his tradition. His fresh translation of the Greek New Testament was one of several books that would have a great influence on the reformers.

But it was Martin Luther that would ultimately get the most attention. Luther was a well-educated monk who taught theology in Wittenberg. Burdened by the guilt of his sins, he searched for a better understanding of salvation. By Luther's day, the church of Rome was teaching that people could earn favor with God by praying to saints or giving money to the church or performing other good works. But as Luther began to study, his *convictions* or beliefs changed. By reading the books of Augustine, the sixth-century African bishop, he saw that grace is something God gives to sinners because they cannot earn salvation by their works. By studying the Apostle Paul's letter to the Romans, Luther saw that no person could appear righteous before God unless that person has faith in Christ. Luther concluded that eternal life is by grace alone through faith alone in Christ alone.

Luther's conclusions stirred up controversy. His teachings directly challenged the authority of the pope and the Roman church. As a priest, Luther hoped to reform the church from the inside, the way Christians had done for centuries with church councils. But to his great disappointment, he was labeled a *heretic*, or false teacher, and *excommunicated*, or kicked out of, the church. He continued to protest false doctrines from outside the established church, leading to the formation of the *Protestant* church.

Many other priests and theologians felt the time was right for reform, and they supported Luther's efforts. When his life was threatened, powerful political leaders kept him safe and gave him opportunities to publish books, including the first modern translation of the Bible into German.

THE BELIEFS OF THE REFORMERS

Luther and other reformers emphasized that sinners are righteous before God by grace alone through faith alone because of Christ alone. They argued that because of Christ's work on the cross, all Christians can approach God directly and do not need a priest to mediate for them. They believed that the only authority for doctrine and practice is Scripture, not the pope.

Many reformers believed that the medieval popes had come to abuse their power. At first, they just wanted to reform the pope's role. But they soon decided that the idea of just one man as God's representative over the whole earth was unbiblical. Some reformers went so far as to call the pope the antichrist, warned of in the Bible.

With so many doctrines being challenged at once, it is not surprising that the reformers did not always agree with each other on every point.

One of the main disagreements they had was over the Lord's Supper. Is it just a ceremony to remind us of Jesus' death, or does something spiritual happen when we take the bread and wine? They never agreed on the details, but they did agree that taking the Lord's Supper is one of the most important acts of obedience for Christians.

Though the reformers believed the Christian tradition needed correction, they did not turn their backs on all the believers who had come before them. They had great respect for the ancient church fathers and medieval theologians who had built the church over the centuries. They often quoted these earlier Christians in support of their reforms.

MULTIPLE REFORMATIONS

As others from across Europe added their voices to Luther's, the Protestant Reformation spread rapidly.

In the Swiss city of Zürich, a priest named Ulrich Zwingli led the Reformation. At a time when many priests never even read the New Testament, Zwingli was shocked at what he saw as superstition in the church. His convictions were similar to Luther's, though the two never agreed on everything. But as Luther's teachings began to spread, Zwingli gained the support of Zürich and he broke with the church of Rome.

In the Swiss city of Geneva, the adopted home of second-generation French reformer John Calvin, the Reformation was a long and difficult process. Calvin, a lawyer, joined forces with Guillaume Farel to reorganize the relationship between the church and the state government in Geneva. His manual for Christians, *The Institutes of the Christian Religion*, influenced generations of Christians throughout Europe and is still considered one of the most important contributions of the reformers.

Calvin's influence was felt in many countries. In Scotland, the Reformation was led by John Knox, who had spent time with Calvin in Geneva while exiled from Scotland. In France, the French Calvinists or *Huguenots* struggled for the right to worship as Reformed Christians. Led by leaders like Queen Jeanne of Navarre, the price of their freedom was war with the king.

In Italy and Spain, reform was led by theologian Juan de Valdéz (ca. 1500-1541), Bernardino Ochino (1487-1564), and Peter Martyr Vermigli (1500-1562). All three were influenced by the reformers, especially Martin Bucer in Strasbourg and Ulrich Zwingli in Zürich. Many, including Vermigli, faced serious opposition by the authorities in Rome and were forced to flee early in the Reformation.

In England, the Reformation officially began when King Henry VIII separated the English church from Rome because the pope refused to grant him a divorce from his first wife. English Christians took the opportunity to push for reform. Thomas Cranmer, the Archbishop of Canterbury, and Queen Katherine Parr, Henry's sixth wife, encouraged the king to accept Reformation doctrines. The Reformation in England would be a long struggle as the kings and queens after Henry shifted the country back and forth between Catholic and Protestant loyalties.

A significant aspect of the English Reformation was the push to produce a Bible in the language of the common people. In the fourteenth century, John Wyclif translated the Bible into English, but it was never published. In 1526, William Tyndale (ca. 1494-1536) published an English New Testament. The most famous English translation of the period was authorized by King James I. Published in 1611, the *King James Version* was the dominant version for nearly 400 years.

RADICAL REFORMATION

Some Protestants felt that the reformers had not taken the changes far enough. They argued that there were even more doctrines of the church, such as infant baptism, that also needed correction. They were called *Anabaptists* (meaning "re-baptizers") because they insisted that people who had been baptized as babies be baptized again as adults after they professed Christ. Some of the early Anabaptist leaders threatened to kill Catholics and fellow Protestants who would not convert to their view. Because of their extreme views, their movement has often been labeled the *Radical Reformation*. But under the leadership of men like Menno Simons, they adopted a peaceful approach to reformation. Today, their most well-known followers are the Mennonites and the Amish.

FINDING THE TRUE STORY

These are the stories of real Christians, told in a way that helps us understand how they saw their world and their calling to reform the church. How do we know what they thought? The reformers wrote thousands of letters and books! Like all imperfect people, their zeal for their cause led them to exaggerate the facts. Sometimes they portrayed their opponents in the worst possible light. Sometimes they glossed over their friends' faults. Sometimes their accounts leave out important information. To find the truth, we have to read their writings and other documents of their time carefully.

With courage and conviction, these Christians declared their devotion to the authority of Scripture. They faced off against the most powerful leaders of the known world. They endured torture and martyrdom for the freedom to worship according to their consciences. From German castles to French battlefields and over the high seas to the Americas, join us as we voyage into the world of the Reformation.

DESIDERIUS ERASMUS: THE HEN THAT LAID THE EGG OF LUTHER

JULY 10, 1520. CALAIS.

FLAGS FURLED AND snapped above the tents as raindrops spurted from the gray skies. On one side of the camp, banners identified the rain-stained tents of Charles V, Holy Roman Emperor. On the opposite side flew the emblems of Henry VIII, King of England. Between them on the hill stood a large square tent, one side rolled up into a wide entrance.

Inside stretched a long table. King Henry, tall and barrel-chested, sat at one end, facing the slim young Emperor Charles. At the emperor's elbow stood a middle-aged man in a black cloak and cap. He listened quietly, his broad lips pressed together in concentration. His gaze remained fixed on the counselor at Henry's side, who stood straight and tall with his hands clasped behind him.

The talks had come to a successful close. Both rulers set their seals on the treaty before them. Rising, they shook hands and exited the tent, departing in opposite directions. The soldiers and members of their courts filed out behind them.

Soon the two legal advisors were alone in the big room, the wet canvas flapping in the wind outside.

"It has been a long time!" cried Henry's advisor, Sir Thomas More, pulling his friend into a hearty embrace.

"Far too long," agreed the black-capped Desiderius Erasmus, his voice vibrating as Thomas thumped him on the back. "But what happy circumstances bring us together now!"

"Peace is a worthy legacy, eh, my friend?"

"For peace, I will venture even into this rain. God must have provided it so you would not be homesick for England."

Thomas laughed. "Do you not miss our English rains?" He carried a chair from one end of the table to the other and they sat down together.

"My days in England are among my fondest memories, but the rain I can do without."

"My home is at your disposal anytime you can visit." Thomas pulled a bundle of paper from inside his vest. "Here. I had started a letter to you when I received word we would meet on this field."

"Thank you. Are you still collecting coins?" asked Erasmus.

"Of course."

"I acquired these from a friend." He produced a silk pouch from the pocket tied inside his robe and emptied six Roman coins into Thomas's hand.

"Ah! They're exquisite!" Thomas beamed at him. "How thoughtful of you."

Erasmus leaned forward with a look of conspiracy. "So. I understand this was not your first treaty in this field."

"Your source is correct," said Thomas, chuckling. "We met with King Francis near here only a month ago. But it is no secret, even if the rumors are a bit outlandish."

"Some say the two kings were so happy to see each other that they danced through the field," said Erasmus, leaning back in his chair.

Thomas laughed. "Like I said, the rumors exaggerate!"

"But it was more than a simple treaty talk," insisted Erasmus. "The meeting is being called the Field of Cloth of Gold."

Thomas nodded. "It was full of pomp and extravagance, all Cardinal Wolsey's idea. Our good friend John Fisher believes he could find at least two sermons' worth of material from the excesses displayed there! I've never seen so much feasting, jousting, and dancing. Both kings nearly went bankrupt showing off their treasures. They even had a man who could put both legs behind his head and walk on his arms."

Erasmus rolled his eyes with disdain. "Some people pick strange careers."

Thomas leaned in. "The secret is that the meeting was an expensive failure. Wolsey tells the story differently, of course, but the truth is that Francis challenged Henry to a wrestling match." He paused for effect. "Henry lost more than his temper."

Erasmus's eyebrows shot up. "It would take a powerful man to out-wrestle Henry! What happened?"

"Sorry, I am sworn to secrecy," Henry grinned. "You know how it is for us royal counselors." But his smile quickly faded. "However, there is something pressing we must discuss."

Erasmus shuffled in his chair. "You speak of Luther."

"Yes. The monk who will be the death of us all." Thomas shook his head in disapproval. "It is always the monks who cause trouble."

"I was a monk," reminded Erasmus.

"You make my point!" said Thomas, grinning again. "You hated being a monk, but you're still a troublemaker. Your most recent book does nothing but mock the monastic orders."

"Monasteries are full of hypocrites and greedy fiends," declared Erasmus, jabbing a finger in the air for emphasis.

"Well, yes, and I've had plenty of letters from monks asking me never to associate with you again."

"I do hope you don't listen to them."

"I do not," assured Thomas. "But if you put your support behind this Luther, you put yourself at risk. He is seeking your support, isn't he?"

"He is," Erasmus admitted. "And he's sharp. But he is not as bad as people say. He just wants to reform the church as many of us do."

"My friend, I know that you desire reformation in the church more than most, but you do not want to be entangled with this rebellious man. The pope has issued an edict against him!"

"I read it," said Erasmus, rolling his eyes again. "The pope calls him 'a wild boar invading the vineyard.' Colorful language indeed."

"Your name is being associated with his. If you are not careful, you could find yourself facing the pope's anger, too."

"My edition of the Greek New Testament was dedicated to the pope," reminded Erasmus. "He won't soon forget that."

"The pope has a short memory for those who oppose him."

"You have to admit that Luther is right in many ways," insisted Erasmus. "He is pointing the church back to the gospel and away from corruption and political ambitions. He teaches faith in Christ alone. How can we argue with that?"

Thomas squinted at him. "Are you a Lutheran?"

Erasmus stood abruptly. "I am a Christian. I cannot help it if Luther has found my appeals for change helpful to his cause. But I do not claim to agree with everything he says or does. I believe in the unity of the church first. Truth must be spoken, but the way it is spoken is just as important. I recently told Luther's friend Melanchthon that I pray Christ will temper Luther's pen. He has a lot of good to say, but his emotions get in the way."

"I mean no harm with my questions, Erasmus," said Thomas, rising and putting a hand on the other man's shoulder. "I simply do not wish to see you dragged into this mess. I'm afraid one of these days you will be asked to choose a side on the Luther matter."

Erasmus shrugged. "I can't imagine why my opinion on Luther counts in the first place."

"Don't underestimate your influence. Your opinion on everything counts to many powerful people."

Erasmus adjusted his cap and turned to the tent flap. "I must return to the university tomorrow, but it has been good to see you, my friend. We must talk again."

"Indeed." Thomas smiled and raised a hand in farewell.

The mud squished under his boots as Erasmus made his way back to Charles's camp. As he descended the hill, a boy approached with a message. "The emperor calls for you, Master Erasmus." He followed the messenger to the emperor's tent.

Charles looked up with a smile as he entered. "Come in, my friend."

The counselor shook the rain from his cap and drew near the emperor's writing table. Maps and military rosters and the newly-signed treaty were spread out across the smooth surface.

Charles was only nineteen when he became emperor a year ago, and Erasmus was not afraid of him. Oh, he had no doubt about the emperor's absolute power—Erasmus knew he was capable of dangerous things—but he also knew that Charles acted out of youthful conviction. He sought the approval of the pope and grew more zealous for the church every day. The church's assistance would be indispensable in restoring the old Roman empire.

"Today we have signed a treaty with England," said Charles with a toss of his dark curls. "Now the French have even more reason to reconsider war with the empire. Thank you for your counsel in these matters."

Erasmus bowed. "I am pleased to be at your service, Sire. It is a privilege to help maintain the peace of the empire."

"You do despise war, don't you?"

"I believe in the unity of the church and the nation. Wars are for those who cannot persuade with the mind."

"Good," the emperor nodded approvingly. "I didn't think you would disrupt the peace of the church by helping the cause of that heretic Luther."

Erasmus was silent.

Charles rose and came around from behind his desk, leaning against it and crossing his arms. His riding breeches and boots were spattered with mud. He had tossed his cloak over his chair, but still wore an embroidered vest, and under it, a high-collared blouse with full sleeves.

"I am aware that you are being pressured from both sides to decide where you stand on this reformation business," he said evenly. "I want you to know that I believe you will stand with the church."

Erasmus squared his shoulders. "I have always stood with the church, even as I have sought reform."

"Everyone wants some kind of reform, but this radical monk Luther is out to destroy the divinely established order of the church of Christ!"

"You have my word that I seek no such thing."

Charles studied the face of his counselor and then turned away, apparently satisfied. "You are returning to the Netherlands? Back to Louvain?"

"My university duties await—unless Your Highness requires my further service."

The emperor waved a hand and returned to his seat. "I will send for you when I have need. But, Erasmus—." His eyes were serious again. "You are far more brilliant than Luther. Consider your decisions carefully. He has been excommunicated and I am about to call a hearing in Saxony at the request of his protector, the Elector Frederick. I would not like your name to be involved."

Erasmus bowed a second time. "I hope that your hearing will result in a fruitful discussion and a peaceful solution, my lord."

"Good day, Master Erasmus."

Back at his university office a few weeks later, Erasmus brushed the dust from his chair and sorted through the pile of letters that had arrived while he was away. A publisher in Venice wanted to publish his next manuscript. A French bishop thanked him for loaning him a book and wondered if he could send another. The headmaster of a school in Germany sought his advice. He stacked the letters on a corner of his desk to reply later.

But there were more letters to open. Three were from scholars at other universities calling on him to write against the Lutheran teachings. Two others demanded that he use his political influence to defend Luther. The last one was from someone he had never met, declaring that if he joined Luther in overthrowing the pope, he would also join Luther in eternal condemnation!

"Thomas More is right. This monk is going to be the death of us all!" he muttered, and shoved the whole pile of letters off the desk. A puff of dust swirled up from the floor. He watched it spin in the morning sunlight slanting from the window.

Getting down on the floor, he reached into the shadows under his desk and pulled out a box. It was full of letters. The ones on top were dated several months ago. The ones on the bottom were dated several years ago. Each page was written in the same angular handwriting, and at the close of each was the same signature— Martin Luther.

He rifled through the letters. Luther wanted to know how he interpreted a passage of Scripture. Luther wanted him to explain why he written something in one of his books. Luther wanted him to be more vocal in calling for reform.

"Why do I even keep these letters?" he asked himself.

Perhaps he could convince the monk to be more careful for everyone's sake. He slid the box back under his desk and sat down again. Opening a jar of ink and dipping in his pen, he began to write across a clean sheet of paper.

August 1, 1520. To the Reverend Doctor Martin Luther: Greetings. You have asked my opinion on recent matters, but there are better persons in this world to give you advice. The king of England once asked me what I thought of you. I told him that I had far too little learning to judge a scholar of your caliber. He told me that he wished you wrote with more moderation of temper. All of us who agree with your purpose wish you would follow that advice. It is a serious matter to challenge men who can only be overthrown by violence, and I fear that blood will be shed because of you. You would do well to focus your writings on Scripture and keep your personal feelings out of them. Farewell, dearest brother in the Lord.

He snatched up his cap and hurried out to send the letter.

Summer wore on. Erasmus spent most of his time studying the books of Hebrews and James, editing a new edition of the works of Saint Augustine, and replying to the stacks of mail that arrived every week. He hoped to hear that Luther had taken his advice.

Instead, he received a package of pamphlets Luther had written criticizing priests and urging German nobles to stand up to the pope. Erasmus shook his head sadly. It was only a matter of time now, he knew. The empire stood on the brink of war.

Early one evening in the fall, he was hunched over his desk when he heard hoofbeats clattering across the courtyard outside his window. Moments later, an urgent knock came at his door. He heard the knock repeated across the hall.

He threw open the door. A student was already down the corridor knocking at another office.

"What is all the commotion?" he demanded.

"I beg your pardon, Master Erasmus. Girolamo Aleandro is here. The faculty are asked to meet him downstairs."

Erasmus started. "Did you say Aleandro?"

"Yes. The pope's messenger says he has an important message for the university." The boy continued down the corridor, pounding on doors.

Erasmus withdrew to his office and put a hand over his eyes. "This whirlwind of Luther will destroy everything in its path!" He pulled on his overcoat, shut his door firmly, and marched down the stairs.

Daylight was fading in the courtyard, the university walls casting broad shadows on the cobblestones. Several of his colleagues were clustered around the visitor.

He slowed his pace, frowning, and turned when he heard rapid footsteps behind him. He ran into the shoulder of Nicolaas Egmondanus, a fellow faculty member.

"Excuse my haste," said Nicolaas. "I hear Aleandro brings a message from the pope."

Erasmus just nodded.

"Weren't you once friends?" Nicolaas prodded. "I find it curious that your former friend is now a trusted representative of the pope even as the pope questions your loyalty."

Erasmus glared at him. Nicolaas made a habit of taunting him.

"Oh, come now, surely the great Erasmus doesn't hold grudges?"

"If I did, I wouldn't be talking to you." He turned away.

Nicolaas followed him. "I hear the pope is excommunicating Luther and sent Aleandro here to ask for our support. I would be prepared. The faculty are likely to condemn Luther and support the pope."

"They would support the devil if he wore flowing white robes," Erasmus muttered.

"I beg your pardon?"

"I said you smell like a sheep herder," he said louder. "Think about it, Nicolaas. Threats and even death did not silence Wyclif and Hus. Why would they silence this monk?"

"Luther will be stopped!" Nicolaas charged off to meet Aleandro.

Erasmus shook his head at the men gathered in the gloomy courtyard. "Slaves to their own self-advancement," he said to himself. "If they loved the peace of the church, they wouldn't run headlong into war with Luther." He decided to go back to his office. There was no point in having words with Aleandro tonight.

Over the next few days Aleandro held meetings with the professors at Louvain. By the end of the week, the faculty had agreed to stand against Luther—except for Erasmus—which meant they would be standing against Erasmus, too. They burned Luther's books in a large bonfire in the courtyard that night.

Luther's whirlwind had struck Louvain.

For the next month, Erasmus kept to himself. He rarely left his office, let most of his mail pile up, and said little to his fellow professors. "Very busy," he said quickly as he passed them in the corridors. "Working on a new book." He spent all of his time bent over the papers on his desk.

One Sunday morning in late October, Erasmus entered the church quietly just as the service was about to begin. He spotted an empty seat at the back and took it. Then he noticed that Nicolaas Egmondanus was seated up front near the pulpit.

"He's preaching today?" Erasmus thought with dismay. Well, he wasn't going to abandon the worship of the Lord today just because he didn't want to hear Nicolaas preach. So he settled into his chair and prayed along quietly with the bishop in Latin. But when Nicolaas went to the pulpit, he let his mind wander back to the Luther problem.

He was thinking of a letter he might write to Luther's friend Melanchthon when he was startled to hear his name shouted from the pulpit. He suddenly realized the other worshipers were staring at him.

Nicolaas swaggered behind the pulpit. "Erasmus is the hen that laid the egg of Luther!" he shouted, thrusting a pointed finger in the air. "Erasmus has been demanding changes in the church for a long time, and has even published an unnecessary new translation of the New Testament. This Luther has fallen for his novelties. But you, people of God, should hold fast to the ancient gospel the church has preserved." He leaned across the pulpit and lowered his voice dramatically. "If these two don't end their challenges to the church, both of them will find their last messages written with the torch!"

Erasmus snatched up his cap and marched out of the church. He was burning with anger. The chilly breeze outside took his breath away, but he set out for a long walk to clear his head.

His fellow professors were publicly denouncing him now. That meant his teaching position was at stake. Thomas More had been right. They were going to force Erasmus to choose a side on the Luther matter. "Why must I be involved?" he shouted to the empty road.

He was glad he was leaving in a few days to attend the emperor's coronation in Cologne. "I have no reason to stay here," he decided. "It is a blessing that my leave is coming so soon. Maybe in a few months this will all be over and I can return in peace."

He went back to the university and slipped up to his office to pack for his journey.

Within a month, he was in Cologne for the coronation. The city was full of feasting and tournaments. Buglers and marching flag-bearers announced the ceremony. Erasmus looked around at the crowd of dignitaries. Everyone was there in their finest clothing to pay their compliments to Charles. All the German princes were there, including Elector Frederick the Wise, Luther's protector. Aleandro was there, too. Erasmus avoided him.

When he went back to his guest room at Count von Neuenahr's house later that night, he had an idea. "I am here with some of the most powerful men in the empire," he thought. "This may be my only chance to persuade them to bring the Luther matter to a peaceful end."

He set a candle on the writing desk by his bed and began to draft a plan. "The key to the solution is getting the three most powerful rulers—Emperor Charles, England's King Henry and

France's King Louis——to consider the matter together. If each sent respected scholars, neutral on the matter, to talk with Luther, the pope would have to listen to them. I know if they just talked to him they could work it all out."

His heart began to race with excitement as his pen flew across the page. But then he realized that if he proposed this plan, they would believe he was a supporter of Luther. Nicolaas's threat might come true. Suddenly he felt paralyzed. The moment of decision had come, as Thomas had warned him.

"What is my duty as a Christian?" he asked himself. "My security, or the peace of the bride of Christ?" The answer was clear. He set his pen firmly to the paper again, and took comfort that he was staying true to his conscience. "This will be my peace treaty, for the good of the church and the lives of innocent people!"

He spent the next two days circulating his plan among the royalty. If they would support it, it might be possible. He soon heard that the German princes were interested in his plan.

On the second night, he returned to his room late. Aleandro was sitting at his desk.

Erasmus suddenly felt sick to his stomach. A visit from the pope's legate rarely meant good news. "What are you doing here?" he demanded.

Aleandro stood and unrolled a sheaf of papers in his hand. "Do you know what this is?"

Erasmus glanced at the top page. "It is a proposal for peace," he replied. "You might have heard of the concept if you weren't so busy starting your own personal wars."

Aleandro gave a hard laugh. "Erasmus, wit has always been your strong point, but politics is mine."

"Surely you agree that peace is better for the church."

"You are proposing that these independent scholars instruct the pope," said Aleandro, now pacing the room. "Instruct the pope!"

"Receiving wise counsel does not lessen the pope's authority any more than when you give him advice yourself."

Aleandro stopped pacing. He loved to hear others acknowledge his importance.

"Look, Aleandro. I know how serious this matter is. If the pope concedes to other scholars on some points, it will make him look reasonable," Erasmus argued. "More importantly, it will advance the truth and peace of the Christian world."

Aleandro re-rolled the documents. "The pope has already spoken on this issue. He has declared Luther a heretic and excommunicated him from the church. There is nothing more to be said."

"Are you so bound to the pope that you cannot do the right thing?"

Aleandro flung the door open. "Face it, old man, you just wish you had his ear as I do!"

Erasmus ran out after him. "If you'd give him back his ear, maybe he could listen to reason!"

He turned to go back into his room. But then he noticed a tall man standing in the shadowy corridor a few paces away. Erasmus started to say something, but the man raised a finger to his lips. They waited for the ringing of Aleandro's footsteps to fade. Then the stranger motioned for Erasmus to follow him.

"Now what?" Erasmus wondered. It had been a long night already. But he had a strong feeling he should go with this man.

He followed him to the end of the corridor, down the stairs, and out of the house through the servants' entrance. They cut through the kitchen garden, where frost-damaged vines lay curled and silent in the darkness. An iron gate opened onto a narrow street. The stranger moved quickly past stone walls and several gates like the one they'd exited. He stopped abruptly in front of one, swung it open noiselessly, and they were in another garden. A dim light burned in a first floor window as they approached a house. Erasmus suddenly found himself in an empty room.

"Wait here," the man said, and vanished.

Immediately Erasmus regretted following him. "This is it!" he thought. "Luther's enemies are going to kill me. Why do I let my curiosity get the better of me?"

A door on the other side of the room opened, and he could see into a connecting room lined with books. A figure stepped into the doorway. He had a full head of white hair and a fur cloak around his shoulders. Erasmus recognized him at once.

"Welcome, Master Erasmus. I trust Chancellor Spalatin did not frighten you?"

"It is an honor to meet Elector Frederick the Wise, protector of Martin Luther."

The old man chuckled. "I prefer to think of myself as the protector of all Saxony. But, of course, Luther has made himself require more protection than my other subjects!" He gestured for Erasmus to follow him into the inner room, and they sat down before a modest fireplace.

"Tell me," said the elector, settling his cloak around him. "Did you have a good discussion with Aleandro? I assume he was strutting his feathers everywhere?"

"That is what he does best, good prince."

Frederick smiled, but his eyes grew serious. "I find myself in a predicament. But I have the good fortune to be visiting the same city as the emperor's counselor. Perhaps you would indulge me with a bit of advice?"

Erasmus nodded.

"No one likes men like Aleandro. He thinks he runs the world, but the truth is that the world is running him. He has lost his conscience."

"Indeed."

The elector picked up a sheet of paper from the table beside his chair and handed it to his visitor. "Before I arrived here for the coronation, Aleandro intercepted my caravan to deliver this letter from the pope. He's demanding that I turn over Luther to Rome immediately and that I burn all of his books in my territories."

Erasmus scanned the document quickly.

"If Luther steps foot in Rome, he will never return to Saxony. I know in my heart they will have him killed without a trial."

Erasmus handed the letter back. "I'm afraid you may be right."

Frederick looked at him to continue.

"Luther is a good man," said Erasmus. "The problem is not what he says, but how he says it."

"He's a firebrand, there is no doubt. But I have read your proposal. You must not believe that his words are worthy of death?"

"Luther sinned gravely by striking out against the crown of the pope and the bellies of the monks. Many of us seek reform in the church, but we do not declare our leader the antichrist!" Erasmus sighed. "But I do find the bull of excommunication against Luther quite out of keeping with the gentle character of Christ's vicar. And Luther has asked only for a fair trial and open discussion about what he has written. Why should he not be granted that?"

"It seems it would be best for all of us, including Emperor Charles, if this matter could be settled peacefully."

"I have already said as much to the emperor. But all I can do is give advice. I do not have the power of a prince to make it happen."

"I cannot stop this revolution any more than you can. But a man's life and the peace of the church is at stake. I must be responsible for the little part God calls me to play." The elector's eyes glittered. "Aleandro may have the pope, but I have Luther."

"What will you do about the pope's letter?"

"I'm going to decline his invitation to Rome."

"I don't believe it was an invitation."

"My dear Erasmus," said Frederick with a smile, "you have a lot to learn about politics."

Erasmus shook his head. "You are the second person to tell me that tonight!"

Frederick stood and reached out to shake his guest's hand. "It has been good to talk to you. You are the wise man others say you are."

The tall figure of Chancellor Spalatin appeared in the doorway.

"Spalatin will escort you back to the count's house. No one will know about our meeting tonight." The elector put a hand on Erasmus' shoulder and guided him toward the outer room. "Know this," he said as they parted. "I am loyal to the emperor. But I will do everything in my power to protect Luther's life for as long as God allows."

Erasmus bowed respectfully.

As he followed the silent Spalatin back through the dark maze of gardens, he considered the elector's words. The empire was on the threshold of a bloody revolution that could not be stopped. But at least he had helped save one man's life.

Shortly after his meeting with Frederick in Cologne, Erasmus returned to the university in Louvain. He supported Luther as much as he could without supporting what he believed would lead to the disunity of the church and war. His fellow professors harassed him for being a supporter of Luther, while Luther accused him of loving peace more than truth! He chose his words carefully and kept writing theology books. He died in July 1536, believing there was nothing more he could do to direct the Reformation toward peaceful ends.

Martin Luther: A Conscience Captive to the Word of God

MAY 1521. GERMANY, ON THE ROAD TO ERFURT.

THE WOODS FADED into darkness as the sun disappeared behind the trees. Soon only moonlight illuminated the forest path, the nighttime shadows mimicking the shapes of unnatural beasts. A light wind skittered through the trees. The night was quiet except for the snapping of twigs under horses' hooves and the rhythmic squeaking of wagon wheels.

The occupants of the wagon rode in silence. Traveling through the woods at night was dangerous—especially if your cargo was a convicted heretic.

In the wagon bed, the heretic sat with his eyes closed, trying to rest. He hadn't slept in days, and with the wagon bouncing as it was, it was obvious he wouldn't be sleeping tonight either. A chilly gust of night air made him shiver. He bundled up some of his books in his cloak, hoping to block the wind.

He jumped when a screeching cry and a fluttering of wings barreled through the branches above the trail. "What was that, Amsdorf?" he said in a loud whisper.

"It was the devil coming for you, heretic," growled Amsdorf from the corner of the wagon, where he was serving as sentry.

A third man shook his head. "It was just a hawk," said Petzensteiner, shifting on the rough wooden planks. "And no more talking. Voices carry in the woods at night."

The heretic settled back into his corner and pulled his hood over his face, feeling his heart rate slow as his eyes grew heavy. He was drifting into uncomfortable sleep when he heard the rush of hoofbeats and the shouts of riders.

The carriage jerked to a sudden halt, throwing the heretic forward and shaking him awake. In the moonlight he could just make out that they had stopped in a clearing next to the ruins of a tiny chapel. Dark figures on horses surrounded the wagon.

"Where is the heretic?" shouted one of the riders.

The heretic shrank back in the corner. Amsdorf unsheathed his knife.

"I said, where is Martin Luther?" the hooded rider demanded again. His band of horsemen closed in on the wagon, and now they could see a dozen crossbows pointed at their heads.

The wagon driver wrenched around in his seat. "There! That's him!" he cried, pointing a shaking finger at the man behind him.

The heretic drew himself to his feet in the wagon. "I am Martin Luther. And you, sir, are in danger for stopping this transport, as I have been guaranteed safe passage by the emperor."

"There has been a change of plans," replied the horseman. "We will take you the rest of the way."

"My friends are armed," Martin warned.

"I see the little knife this one is clutching," he said with a laugh. "Perhaps your friend thinks his dagger is faster than a crossbow?" He turned on his horse. "Grab the heretic and his condemned books!" he ordered his men.

With bows pointed at their chests, Amdorf and Petzensteiner could only watch as the horsemen plucked Martin from the wagon.

Martin kicked and shouted as they tied up his legs and arms. They shoved a hood over his head and hoisted him onto a horse.

In moments the woods were quiet again. Martin's friends were left staring at each other.

"Get this wagon moving!" Petzensteiner shouted to the driver. "Take us to the closest village so we can form a search party."

Martin bounced on the back of the horse for hours. They crossed open fields, splashed through streams, and tore through forests. Finally, they stopped. Martin could hear the chains of a drawbridge lowering and the clatter of cobblestones as his horse crossed to the other side. By then, Martin was so sore that he slid to the ground as soon as they untied his legs.

"Get up, heretic. We're not carrying you up those stairs!" his captors declared.

At the top of the stairs, Martin's hood was removed. After the darkness of the shroud, he blinked in the light of a single candle. It took a moment for his eyes to refocus. He recognized the amused face staring back at him.

"Hans von Berlepsch? Is that you?"

Hans chuckled. "Welcome to Wartburg Castle, Herr Luther. I am so pleased this good knight could deliver you safely."

"Glad to be of service, Herr von Berlepsch," said the knight with a bow.

"He could have done it less painfully!" said Martin, rubbing his shoulder. "Does the elector know I'm here?"

"Elector Frederick knows you're safe, but not that you're right here in his own castle," explained Hans. "He had to be believable when he told the pope's legate, Aleandro, that he had no idea where you were."

"Spalatin wouldn't even tell *me* where I was going," said Martin.

Hans shrugged. "It was for your own protection. After your safe passage by the emperor expires, you will be facing any number of men dying to make a name for themselves. You would have been executed."

The knight walked to the door. "I have never enjoyed a prank so much!" he declared. "You are a good actor, Herr Luther." He disappeared down the stairwell.

"By tomorrow morning, everyone will believe you are dead," said Hans.

"Even Amsdorf?"

"Amsdorf was one of the few who were in on our plan."

Martin remembered Amsdorf's quick hand on his knife. "He was very convincing. I guess he's not rounding up a search party."

Hans laughed. "The only search he's doing is for a tavern where he can get a well-deserved drink."

Martin noticed a stack of books and paper next to the candlestick on the table. "What happens now?"

"This is to be your home for some time, Martin." Hans tossed him a bundle of clothes. "Change into these. And you are not to leave this room until your tonsure and beard have grown in. We can't risk anyone recognizing you."

"What if someone wanders up here?"

"The stairwell is retractable, so you shouldn't have any surprises. But if you do, your name is now Knight George. I'll see that any letters you write are delivered, but don't use your real name and don't give any clues about your location."

"So this castle is to be my Patmos, then? I'm in exile like the Apostle John?"

"Focus on the positive, Martin."

"What might that be?" Martin demanded.

Hans raised an eyebrow at him. "You're not dead."

Martin grunted.

Hans pointed to the books. "Oh, and you'll have plenty of time to work on your German Bible translation without the interruptions of politics."

Martin glanced at the book titles, but shoved them aside impatiently. "If that is to be my occupation, then I will need more books than these."

"Give me a list tomorrow then."

"And more paper. I write fast."

"Chancellor Spalatin will be here in a few days and he'll get you whatever supplies you need," Hans assured him. "But now, I suggest you rest. You've had a most exciting night for a monk!"

"I've had a most exciting few months," Martin corrected under his breath, as the door shut behind Hans. He quickly changed into the borrowed clothes and, lifting the candle, found the rough bed in the corner.

Lying on his back, he stared up at the shadowy corners of the unfamiliar room. "Exile," he repeated to himself. "All I wanted to do was share the good news of the gospel and now I'm a wanted man hiding in the German countryside."

He remembered his own quest for the gospel. He had been a monk and a theology student in Erfurt. He spent his days praying with the other monks and reading Scripture, but at night he was tormented by his sins. How could he spend eternity with a righteous God when he was so sinful? He longed to know that God had forgiven him, but how could he be sure?

He made a pilgrimage to Rome. With hundreds of other pilgrims, he climbed the stairs at St. Peter's Basilica on his knees. He paused on every step and begged God to forgive his sins. When he reached the top, he turned and looked down over the stairs. His fellow pilgrims prayed desperately, hoping God would notice their bleeding knees and their tears and have mercy. "Is this what God requires of us?" he asked himself. "God is holy and must punish sin, but he is also merciful. If we must bargain with God to forgive us, why did Jesus die?" He returned to Erfurt more confused and depressed than before.

That spring he was sent to Wittenberg to teach theology. For several years, he studied and taught and wrote letters to other scholars. He questioned what the church had taught him about salvation from sin. When he began to study the book of Romans, he found something amazing. "'The just shall live by faith,'" he read excitedly. "The holy Scriptures state that salvation is not by anything I do, but only by faith in Christ." He began to teach this to his students.

The final turning point came when a priest named Johann Tetzel arrived in Germany with a large money chest. In each village, he called the people together to give them a message from Pope Leo. "If you want to save your relatives from the flames of purgatory, give your money to the church," he announced. "When a coin in the coffer rings, another soul from purgatory springs!"

Martin had heard about this Tetzel who was raising money for the pope's building project, but still he could hardly believe his ears. "For a fee, the pope will let us into heaven?" Martin shouted angrily. But the crowd ignored him. He could barely keep his footing as the sea of people surged forward to throw their last coins into the pope's money chest.

"How could the church forget the cross?" thought Martin, shaking his head and backing away from the throng. "The Bible says only the righteousness of Christ brings forgiveness of sins, not giving money to the church. The pope doesn't have the authority to save anyone!"

He knew he had to do something about this error. He went back to his room, got out a large sheet of paper, and spent the rest of the night writing down all the reasons Tetzel and the pope were wrong. By morning, he had written 95 statements in Latin. He nailed the list to the broad wooden door of the church, hoping scholars would read it and respond.

And they did. They argued about it, whispered about it. They even translated it into German and passed it around to the people. Cartoons mocking the pope circulated. Soon the whole countryside was in an uproar.

Martin went on preaching and teaching about the righteousness of Christ. The following year, he published a book called *Resolutions Concerning the 95 Theses*. "Priests can declare that we are forgiven," he wrote, "but they don't have the power to take away our sin. The only thing that saves us is faith in Christ's promise. The church needs a reformation! Such is not the business of the pope or his cardinals, but the business of the whole Christian world and of God alone." He dedicated the book to Pope Leo X.

The pope called for Martin's unqualified surrender as a doctor of the church. Martin refused. He wrote more books, debated with other scholars, denied that he was a heretic. The pope threatened to excommunicate him.

Martin wanted a trial so he could explain in person what was wrong with the church's teachings. He asked his friend Spalatin, secretary to Germany's Elector Frederick the Wise, for help. Elector Frederick was out of sorts with Rome and asked Emperor Charles V to grant Martin a fair hearing. Charles agreed, and promised Martin safe passage to the city of Worms, where the hearing would be held before high-ranking members of the church and the princes of Germany.

The day Martin left for Worms was burned into his memory. Friends gathered with tears in their eyes to say good-bye. "Speak only the truth," urged Melanchthon, Martin's thin friend and fellow professor. "Stand fast."

Martin put his hand on his friend's shoulder. "Even if I die, you must continue to preach the truth about the power of the cross."

Melanchthon shook his head. "God has provided you Frederick the Wise as your protector, Martin. You have been promised safe passage to the council."

"So was John Hus a hundred years ago, and he was burned at the stake! And now the people are calling me the Hus of Saxony!"

"Do not think that way, Martin. Amsdorf is going with you. I believe you will be safe."

But when the small wagon train jerked away, Martin felt sure he would never see Wittenberg again.

Martin and Amsdorf and the rest of their party headed west toward Worms. Martin was shocked at the welcome they received as they passed from town to town. People followed his carriage, waving to him. Whenever he stopped, crowds gathered along the road to hear him preach.

"Stand up for the truth!" they shouted. "Stand up for Germany!"

Amsdorf had to run off the crowds after a time. "Make room for us to pass!" he shouted. "Martin Luther cannot stand up for anything if he never makes it to Worms."

The journey took two weeks. By the time he arrived, the whole city was waiting for him. Trumpets announced his arrival. Hundreds of people gathered to escort him through the city gates. He had barely taken a peek at the room where he would be staying when princes arrived to welcome him.

The whole country was in an uproar about this monk who challenged the pope.

The day of the trial, Martin donned the tunic of his Augustinian order, and had his tonsure cleanly shaven.

At the entrance of the great hall, a line of the emperor's Spanish guards parted to let him pass. The room was full of dignitaries, including the seven electors who governed the emperor's territories. Frederick the Wise and his secretary Spalatin were among them. In the front row, perched on stands, sat representatives of the pope in their scarlet robes and caps. They stared openly at this man who had dared challenge the teachings of the church.

As he reached the center of the meeting hall, he came face-to-face with Emperor Charles seated in his robes. Before him on a low table was a stack of Martin's books.

Chancellor Johann Eck stood and went to the table, pacing before it for a full minute. "Martin Luther, you have been called here to answer two questions." He turned suddenly to face Martin, his arm raised dramatically, his sleeve bunched at his elbow, pointing at the pile of books. "Did you write these books?"

"They are not going to give me my debate," Martin thought with a pang of fear. "I am going to be burned like Hus!"

Eck took a step forward. "Will you recant what you have written here?"

"If you please, Chancellor, let the titles of the books be read out."

Eck frowned, but pawed through the stack, reading each title rapidly. "*On Good Works*, *On the Liberty of a Christian Man*, *Address to the German Nobility*, *Explanation of the Lord's Prayer....*" He went on for several minutes.

"There," he said when he was finished. "Martin Luther, His Holy and Invincible Imperial Majesty has called you to retract these books. Did you write them?"

"The books are mine, and I've written others as well."

"Will you recant them?"

"Because this is a matter of faith and the salvation of souls," said Martin, "I ask for more time to consider."

The emperor's counselors huddled around him to discuss the request. Grumbling arose from the disappointed princes who had expected a show.

Returning to the middle of the floor, Eck faced Martin. "The emperor grants you one day. Make good use of the time. You will be called to return tomorrow."

Martin fled back to his room and fell on his knees by his bed. "Heavenly Father, what am I to do?" His heart was pounding, and the palms of his hands were sweating. He forced himself to concentrate on his prayer instead of his fear.

"I only want to be your faithful servant. You have shown me that I cannot gain my salvation by the pope's decree or buy it from Tetzel. You have shown me not to trust in my own penance, but only in the sacrifice of Christ on the cross. You have shown me that the church has grown corrupt and that the bishops are no longer any different from the lords and nobles who steal from the poor. You must have taught me this for a reason. Surely I am here to do more than die!"

He clasped his hands together to try to keep them from shaking so much, then realized he had stopped praying. His eyes flashed open and he squinted around the darkened room. "Devil, I will not listen to your fear. Stop interrupting my prayers!" he shouted. "So long as Christ is merciful, I will never recant one word." He got to his feet and flung his arms wide. "Use me to bring reform to your church, Lord. Kill me, if you must, but use me!"

He spent the night poring over his books in prayer.

It was evening of the next day when he was summoned back to the hall. Torches flickered along the walls, casting long shadows across the gathered faces. The audience was bigger than the night before.

Martin bowed before the emperor. Chancellor Eck began to speak even before he had risen.

"Martin Luther, His Imperial Majesty has graciously provided you the opportunity to think about your answers before this court. Time has now run out. Did you write these books and will you recant them?" demanded Eck.

Martin turned slowly around the circle of onlookers, his dark eyes glittering in the firelight. He was determined to get his debate. "These are my books," he confirmed, "unless—."

Eck looked up sharply.

"Unless someone has slipped a book into the pile that I did not write."

Eck glared at him and ignored the accusation. "Will you defend these in whole, or is there any part that you wish to recant?" he asked again.

Martin took a deep breath and walked to one end of the table.

"Most Serene Lord Emperor, most illustrious princes," he began. "There are three kinds of books in these stacks. In the first, I've taught on the Christian faith and good works in a clear and proper way. My friends and enemies agree on these teachings, so I cannot recant these."

He moved to stand before the middle of the table. "There are also books I've written against the pope. To recant those would be to encourage his tyranny, so I cannot."

The crowd murmured, but he raised a hand and went to the far end of the table. "The third kind of books are against those who have supported the tyranny of Rome. I admit that the words I used were often too violent and harsh." He paused, and the dignitaries leaned forward in their seats. "While I wish my tone had been different," he continued, "the substance of these books I cannot recant either."

A flurry of whispers ran around the room. Eck's eyes narrowed with impatience. "You must give a simple and proper answer to the question. Will you or will you not recant?"

Martin ground his teeth, frustrated that he could not engage Eck in a debate to explain his teachings. "Very well! Since Your Serene Majesty and your lordships require a simple answer, I will give you one." He folded his arms across his chest and faced Eck squarely. "I do not put my faith in popes or councils alone, who contradict each other and themselves. My conscience is captive to the Word of God. Unless I am convinced by the testimony of the Scriptures, I cannot—I will not—recant anything. For it is neither safe nor right to act against one's conscience."

He turned to the emperor with arms spread. "Here I stand! I can do no other! God help me."

The council debated for several days about what to do with Martin Luther.

"What is taking so long?" Martin demanded, when Spalatin came to visit him in his quarters.

Spalatin handed him a note from Elector Frederick. It read: "Father Martin spoke excellently. He is too bold for me."

"Your supporters and your enemies are both powerful," Spalatin said. "The biggest concern at the moment is that you have the support of the people. Placards with a drawing of a peasant's boot are showing up all over the city."

"The peasants are threatening to revolt against their princes because of me?"

"Not just because of you, but you have certainly inspired them to question the way things are. You've become dangerous."

"I will be declared a heretic, won't I?"

"Yes, of that there is no doubt. The elector tells me that Charles has made it clear he intends to continue to uphold Rome's authority as his forefathers have done."

Martin threw himself on his bed. "Then I am finished!"

"Don't be so dramatic, Martin. You forget that you have powerful friends. You will be excommunicated by the pope, but Charles doesn't want to risk any political uprisings. You are to stop preaching and return directly to Wittenberg. He will guarantee your safe conduct for the next twenty-one days."

"Twenty-one days! What about after that?"

Spalatin grinned and leaned in. "Elector Frederick is not about to lose his favorite professor. We have a plan."

It was Spalatin's wily smile that Martin remembered as he lay on the borrowed bed in a small room in Wartburg Castle.

"So here I am," he thought grimly. "I'm a theology professor for a church that is about to condemn me. I'm a fugitive from the most powerful man in the world. And now I'm stuck here with a few measly books waiting for my hair to grow back in!" He rolled over and buried his face in his sleeve.

When Spalatin arrived a few days later, he found Martin at a table. He was leaning over Erasmus' translation of the Bible and scribbling on a stack of papers.

"So it's true," said Spalatin. "You're as ugly with a beard as you are without it."

Martin looked up in surprise. "Spalatin! How did you get up here?"

"You left the staircase down. Maybe you're not the genius they say you are."

Martin shrugged and took a sack of books from Spalatin's shoulder. "It's about time you got here. Can't do anything without these books. I'm going crazy in here."

Spalatin laughed. "You've only been here for a few days, Martin!"

"That's Knight George to you." Martin glared at him.

"What's so bad about this place? It's quiet, you've got a window and a stack of books, and I see you've already spattered ink all over the wall. You've made it home."

"I'm still bruised from that delightful kidnapping you arranged, and my bowels do not agree with Berlepsch's terrible cooking."

"Your bowels don't agree with anyone's cooking," Spalatin declared. He grabbed a three-legged stool from under the table and sat down. As he did, he pulled out from his vest a flat parcel tied with string.

Martin eyed it. "Is that what I think it is?"

"Yes, the edict of Worms," said Spalatin, handing it over with a frown. "The council has rendered their judgment about you. It's just what you'd expect. You are a heretic, you will be condemned, etc., etc."

Martin unfolded the document on top of his books and scanned it quickly. "If I'm dead, then why does this matter?"

"Most people believe you are dead, but the pope's lawyer Aleandro is no fool. He hopes that you are just in hiding so he can keep chasing you. He called Frederick the Wise a 'cunning fox' and says he's lying about not knowing where you are."

"I'll soon be dead if I have to stay up here!" Martin tore up the edict and set it aflame over the candle on his desk.

"If you try not to burn down the castle first, I'll talk to Berlepsch about getting you out for some fresh air."

"What is the news in the cities?"

"Your death seems to be helping your old friend Karlstadt in Wittenberg," said Spalatin. "He's been itching to lead a rebellion. But the people are suffering as the princes crack down on the rebels. The elector isn't happy with him."

Martin jumped to his feet. "I'll go to Wittenberg and set him straight."

"You are needed here, Knight George," Spalatin reminded him firmly. "If someone recognizes you, you will surely be killed. How can you lead a reformation when you're dead?"

Martin glared at him, but he knew his friend was right, at least for now.

Spalatin rose and put on his cap. "I must return to the elector, but I'll be back, and I'll gladly bring whatever books you need for your translation project." He leaned over the table and tapped a long finger on the stack of paper. "Do what you do well, Martin. Wield your pen for the glory of Christ."

He disappeared down the staircase.

Martin began to sort through the books and letters Spalatin had delivered, then remembered the staircase. With both hands, he turned the crank that retracted the hinged stairs, and shut the door. Back at the table, he found where he had left off in Erasmus's Greek New Testament.

"If tonight's meal is as unsatisfying as last night's, I'll be through this chapter before bedtime!" he muttered, and picked up his quill pen again.

Martin translated the New Testament into German in just eleven weeks in his little cell in Wartburg. He chose his words so carefully that his translation became the basis of the modern German language.

He remained under the imperial ban for the rest of his life, but it didn't stop him from preaching and writing books. He called for his followers to obey their leaders and he called his leaders to obey the Scriptures. He was soon recognized as the greatest leader of a movement that would become known as the Protestant Reformation. Though he did not agree with the other reformers on every interpretation of the Bible, he had a powerful influence on them all.

At the age of forty-two, he married Katarina von Bora, a former nun, and they had six children. He died on February 18, 1546.

THE CATHOLIC REFORMATION

MANY VOICES CALLED for change in the church. Some believed the errors of the Roman church were so bad that they had to separate in protest. Others believed that corrections could only be made if the church was reformed from within. The *Catholic Reformation* was the attempt to do just that. Some Catholic leaders working for reform called themselves "reformers," but after the Protestant Reformation began, they called themselves "Catholic reformers" to distance themselves from people like Luther and Calvin. This movement was not initially a response to the Protestant Reformation, but it became that, so it is sometimes called the *Counter Reformation*.

Some Italian and Spanish reformers, such as Juan de Valdéz and Peter Martyr Vermigli, began as a part of this movement, but because of opposition from other Catholic leaders, they later identified themselves more closely with the Protestant Reformation.

Catholic reformers recognized the political corruption of the church. They saw the leadership of the church as craving power, rather than the spread of the gospel. Many thought it was time to return to the simpler era of early Christianity. Renewed attention to the theology of Augustine and Erasmus fueled the desire for change.

These attempts to reform the church of Rome from the inside took many forms.

Prior to the Protestant Reformation, the Fifth Lateran Council of 1514 was called by Pope Julius II. Martin Luther and other reformers felt it did not bring significant changes to church teachings.

In 1541, some leaders of the Roman church hoped to find some agreement with Protestants. They called a meeting in the city of Regensburg. Protestant delegates included John Calvin, Martin Bucer, and Philipp Melanchthon. The delegates agreed on some issues, but the Protestants and Catholics could not agree on the Lord's Supper and the authority of the pope.

After the failure of Regensburg, Pope Paul III called the Council of Trent (1545-1563). The Council did respond to some abuses by bishops and priests, but its main concern was to clarify the official doctrine of the Catholic church. They wanted to remove false teachings, including those Protestant doctrines they believed were in error. In the end, the Council renewed the teachings of the church which the Reformers saw as contrary to the Bible, and Protestants were specifically condemned.

After the conclusion of the Council of Trent, one of the main goals of the Catholic reformers was to limit the influence of the Protestant reformers. This led to the most infamous aspect of the Catholic Reformation, known as the *Inquisition*. The Inquisition was an organized effort to preserve the teachings of the Roman church against those they identified as heretics. Originally it was a legal investigation into heresy, but the men involved often resorted to bullying, persecution, and censorship of Protestant books. It is hard to know just how cruel the Inquisitors really were, since some Protestant reports are known to be exaggerated. Another measure taken by Catholics to combat Protestant teachings was the founding of a new religious order called the Society of Jesus, led by a former Spanish soldier named Ignatius Loyola. The *Jesuits* were fiercely loyal to the pope. Their efforts to defend the Catholic church against Protestant teachings were quite successful, as they founded schools and aided the poor. Eventually their influence was felt around the world.

Reforming the Catholic church from within proved to be a complicated effort during the sixteenth century.

Menno Simons: A Kingdom of Peace

MARCH 1534. VILLAGE OF WITMARSUM, IN FRISIA.

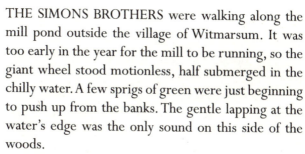

THE SIMONS BROTHERS were walking along the mill pond outside the village of Witmarsum. It was too early in the year for the mill to be running, so the giant wheel stood motionless, half submerged in the chilly water. A few sprigs of green were just beginning to push up from the banks. The gentle lapping at the water's edge was the only sound on this side of the woods.

Menno, the older brother, stopped on the bank and skipped a rock across the pond's surface.

"Leave the priesthood and join me!"

"You make it sound simple."

"It *is* simple."

"No. It is dangerous. It is irresponsible. You know that."

"I don't understand," Peter continued. "You said you were troubled by the state of your soul. Why will you not forsake the pope and join our Anabaptist brothers?"

Menno watched the rock disappear beneath the water, then

turned back to his brother. The family resemblance was strong. Both had dark circles under their eyes and thick eyebrows. Both had long mustaches and pointed beards. But Menno's hair was beginning to recede under his hat.

"I have already made so many changes, Peter," Menno reminded his brother. "I never read the Bible until a few years ago, even in my training for the priesthood. I didn't want to know if the church had gotten it wrong. What would I do if they had? Father wanted me to be a priest, so I became a priest."

He scratched at his nose. "When I finally decided to read the Bible, I had so many questions. So I read the forbidden pamphlets by Luther and Zwingli. I wrote to Bucer in Strasbourg. I became convinced that they are right about the corruption within the church."

Peter held up a hand. "Except that they are wrong about baptism," he interrupted. "Catholics and Reformers all accept infant baptism. But we Anabaptists believe we must be baptized as adults. Luther has not gone far enough in reforming the church."

"Yes," nodded Menno, "and I've come to agree with that as well."

"Then why won't you join me?" asked Peter.

Menno sighed and began to walk along the bank. "Remember what happened to the tailor, Sicke Freerks, when he joined the Anabaptists? He was beheaded! Others are drowned for being rebaptized. It is not a decision to take lightly."

"Perhaps not, but it is the right thing to do."

"What happens to my congregation if I leave or am killed?" Menno insisted. "The church just sends another priest here, one that does not teach the Bible. No, my place is here in Witmarsum, at least for now, as a preacher of the gospel."

Peter frowned and put his hand on his brother's back. "I pray you will find the answers you seek, and that one day you will join us in finishing the work Luther started. But think quickly, my brother, for the end may come soon."

Menno halted and looked up in alarm. "What do you mean?"

"Jan Matthijs has just arrived in Münster," said Peter, excitement dancing in his eyes. "He says he is one of the witnesses prophesied about in the book of Revelation. He says that God will usher in the end of the age and make Münster the New Jerusalem."

"That's ridiculous!" cried the priest. "Melchior Hoffman claimed Christ was going to return last year and set up Strasbourg as the New Jerusalem, but that didn't happen either. Now he's in prison." He shook his head at his brother. "Why do you get involved with these uneducated men?"

Peter folded his arms across his chest. "The Reformation began with men of worldly learning, such as Luther and Erasmus. But God will finish it with men who have no worldly learning. Matthijs and his followers are entirely without learning, and therefore without corruption!"

"All men are corrupt, Peter, because all men are sinners. You are falling into bad company."

"That is Satan speaking, trying to tempt me away from my convictions!" declared Peter. "Well, it won't work. I am going to Münster."

"What?" His brother stared at him.

"The Anabaptists have suffered too long," Peter said. "You yourself mentioned the martyrdom of Sicke Freerks. Matthijs has called us to see that now is the time of harvest. It is time for the Anabaptists to defend themselves against the godless and set up their own city. So I'm going to join them. Wessel the tinker is going with me."

"You've gotten Wessel into this?"

"What do you care about Wessel?"

"He's a member of my congregation." Menno grabbed his brother's arm. "Listen to me, Peter. Radicals that make promises about the end of time are always wrong. They manipulate the poor and use them for their own ambitions. I promise you, this will end in bloodshed."

"Only the ungodly have anything to fear," Peter insisted, setting his chin firmly.

Menno spread his hands wide in exasperation. "Peter——."

"My mind is make up, Menno. We leave tomorrow."

"You are a good brother, but you are a foolish man!" Menno turned away and kicked a clod of dirt into the water. "I see I can't stop you. So go on your pilgrimage, and come back to the village when you see that I've spoken the truth."

Peter and Wessel left for Münster the following day.

Almost immediately, Menno received news that the Anabaptists had taken over the city. But the bishop prince Franz von Waldeck was not going to sit back and give up his city. So his army surrounded them. Peter's New Jerusalem was now under siege.

All Menno could do was pray that Peter and Wessel would be safe.

Summer arrived in the village of Witmarsum. The days grew hot and dusty. Flies gathered around the sheep pens. The village rose early to do their work, rested at midday, then returned to their fields and shops to work until dusk.

At the back of the church, the altar boy, Dirk, was replacing candles and sweeping out the entrance. His soft footsteps and quiet humming were reassuring to Menno, who was on his knees before the altar. The pulpit Bible was open to the twenty-fifth psalm. Menno had spent two hours that morning studying the text before turning to prayer.

Like he did every day, he asked God for wisdom to understand the Scriptures, for rain to water the parched crops, and for the safe return of his brother.

A skirmish at the door brought him suddenly to his feet.

Dirk was bending over to pick up his broom. "Watch it!" he was saying.

"I have to see Father Simons!" A familiar figure ran up the aisle toward him.

"Wessel?" said Menno in surprise. "I remind you that this is the house of the Lord."

"You must hide me, Father. Hide me!" The tinker threw himself at the priest.

"What are you doing here?" Menno said, shaking the young man's hands from his shoulder. "I thought Münster was still under siege."

"It is." Wessel fell to his knees. "Grant me sanctuary, Father. The bishop's troops followed us. If you don't hide me, I'll be arrested!"

Menno glanced toward the door. Dirk had shut it, and with a nod from the priest, he lowered the crossbar to secure it.

"All right," said Menno. "Here, get behind the altar."

Wessel scrambled to wedge himself under the covering.

"Tell me what's going on!" demanded the priest.

"The king sent some of us out of the city—."

"The king? What king?"

"The king! He sent some of us out of the city to round up more troops. I volunteered to go so I could get out of there. It's a terrifying place! I broke away from the others as we approached the village."

"What others?"

A corner of the tablecloth flapped open, and Wessel's face poked out. "The other emissaries of the king! You're not listening to me, Father!"

"Where are the others now?" Menno insisted.

"In the square trying to convince the villagers to join them. They'll proclaim their message until the troops get here and run them off. It's happened in every village between Münster and here!"

"This madness will take no more of my village!" Menno declared. "Stay here, Wessel, and don't make a sound until I get back. I expect you to clear up this nonsense about Münster as soon as I return!"

He snatched up his hat from the last pew. "Dirk, bolt this door when I leave and don't open it until I return. Understood?"

"Yes, Father!"

He dashed up the hill to the square. A stranger was standing in a wagon in front of the inn, shouting. Two men stood nearby, their clothes filthy, their eyes darting expectantly toward the road. Curiosity had driven a few people out of the shops to listen. Conrad, the blacksmith, was leaning in the broad entrance of his smithy.

"I come from Münster," announced the stranger, "and I bring news from the King of the World. All true Anabaptists must leave their worldly possessions and join us in Münster to destroy the unbelievers!"

The crowd looked at him suspiciously.

"That doesn't sound like the gospel I know," the innkeeper dared to reply.

"Then you are ignorant of the true gospel," cried the stranger. "Christ will return, and he will do so in Münster. His Anabaptist servants will establish his kingdom!"

Menno shoved past the crowd and faced the wagon, hands on his hips. "David is right. You, sir, are the ignorant one. What you proclaim is neither the gospel of peace nor the Anabaptist message of Melchior Hoffman."

The stranger rolled his eyes. "Hoffman is in prison because he would not defend himself against his oppressors. The true church cannot live this way any longer. We have suffered enough persecution from those who claim to serve the Lord." He pointed to the crowd. "It is time for you to pick up your swords and usher in the kingdom of God!"

"No!" Menno shouted. "Christ will usher in his kingdom by transforming our hearts, not by us taking up arms against our brothers! Christ's kingdom is a kingdom of peace. Enough of this nonsense."

The stranger leaned in so close Menno could smell his breath. "Who are you to challenge me?"

"I am the priest of this village, and it is my duty to protect these people against false prophets."

The man looked past Menno and continued his call. "One in ten men will die for their defiance against the King of the World. Heed my warning!"

"Get out of this town right now," Menno ordered.

The stranger jumped down from the wagon and shoved him. Menno stood his ground, but refused to fight. The man's two friends closed in on him.

"You don't want to do that," said Conrad, coming forward from the shadow of the smithy, hammer in hand.

Hoofbeats pounded up the road then, and the dogs penned up behind the shoemaker's shop began to howl. The strangers looked at one another in alarm. "Soldiers!" They ran across the square and headed out of the village.

The soldiers had seen their prey scattering toward the woods. The horses didn't even stop in the square but clattered through it and down the road.

Menno glanced at Conrad. The blacksmith just gave him a nod and turned back to his smithy.

"Come on, folks," said the innkeeper, opening the door of his inn. "Come on in and get a drink before you go back to work." A few people followed him inside.

Menno shook his head in dismay and headed back toward the church. "Someone needs to set these Münsterites straight!" he said aloud. "They have zeal, but they are being led astray like ignorant sheep."

Dirk let him into the church, and he convinced Wessel to come out from under the altar.

"The soldiers have come and gone," he explained. "You're safe now."

They sat down in the front pew.

"Tell me what is going on in Münster. Who is this king? Has Matthijs declared himself king?"

"No," said Wessel, gratefully taking the cup of water Dirk brought him. "Matthijs is dead. He was killed on Easter. He declared that if the people had enough faith, Christ would return. To prove it, he led twenty men out of the city gates and charged the bishop's seven thousand troops."

"What? Did he have a death wish?"

The tinker took a long swig from the cup and wiped his mouth on his sleeve. "All twenty of them were slaughtered. Jan of Leiden immediately proclaimed himself king in Matthijs' place." He laughed bitterly. "Oh, Leiden insisted that he was no better than the rest of us, that he was just a swineherd among the people of God. But it is hard to believe a man who has 'King of the World' embroidered on his robes and coins minted with his face!"

Menno shook his head in disbelief.

"Under his reign, all manner of evil has occurred, Menno," Wessel continued. "They burned all books except the Bible. They ordered all the Catholics and Lutherans to convert to Anabaptism or be killed, and then took their possessions. They ordered the men to marry multiple wives so they could have more children. They even took down the church steeples to make room for the canons!"

"What about my brother?" asked Menno quietly. "Is Peter alive?"

"Oh, he's alive. He's one of the twelve elders of Israel."

"I don't understand."

"Leiden abolished the city council and put in their place twelve of his own men that will lead under him like the elders of the twelve tribes of Israel. He gave them each a sword to lead the people into the promised land when Christ returns to Münster."

Menno looked away in embarrassment. "Oh, Peter! How could you be so deluded?"

"The city remains under siege by the bishop's troops. They are running out of food. They are getting sick. I don't know how long they can hold out. That's why Leiden let us leave and try to get past the surrounding troops, so we could bring back reinforcements."

"You're safe now," said Menno. "And your tinker shop is waiting for you. You were right to turn away from this foolishness."

"Thank you, Father." He rose and shook the priest's hand. "I am sorry about your brother."

"So am I," said Menno sadly. "But I'm glad you escaped, Wessel. And I am glad at least to know that Peter is alive."

Wessel nodded, and slipped out of the church. Dirk went back to his cleaning. Menno stayed there on the bench for several hours, praying desperately for his brother.

The rains finally came, and the fields produced a modest crop. The people of Witmarsum busied themselves bringing in the harvest, grinding wheat into flour at the mill, and hanging fresh meat in the smokehouses. Wessel returned to his tinker shop, mending spoons and cooking pots. Every Sunday, the villagers gathered in the bell-topped church at the bottom of the hill to hear Menno preach about repentance and forgiveness.

One autumn day, Menno took his wheelbarrow to the smithy to have the wheel repaired. Stepping inside, his eyes took a moment to adjust from the bright sunlight outside. Conrad loomed over his anvil, sparks flying from a bar of white-hot metal as he pounded it into shape with his hammer. Beyond him, a great oven flickered with blue flames, fed by the giant bellows.

Conrad greeted him and bent to look at the broken wheel. "I'll just need to take this off and replace the spoke. Won't be long."

"Thank you."

The smith yanked on the iron pegs that held the wheel to the wooden body. Menno watched him in silence, feeling the heat of the fire on his face and the smoke stinging his eyes. He decided to wait on a bench near the open door.

"Have you heard from Peter?" Conrad asked him after a few minutes.

"No."

They fell silent again. Menno wondered how Conrad could get used to working over the flames like that. The long leather apron protected his body, but his tough forearms were covered with little scars from the flying sparks. It was a job you had to be born into, Menno decided. If he hadn't become a priest, he would be managing the dairy farm now, herding the cows out in the fresh air.

"I remember milking cows with Peter on my father's farm," he said suddenly. "It wasn't so many years ago. We had our fights, as brothers do, but he was a good boy."

Conrad nodded, his back to Menno. "It is hard to be at odds with one's own flesh and blood."

"I love my brother. I even share his convictions about the Anabaptist doctrine. But I cannot understand the passion and the violence!"

Conrad began to pound out the wheel, and the clanging of metal on metal echoed through the building.

Menno looked up at the doorway in time to see a man ride up on a donkey. His long legs were bent at the knees, his feet nearly dragging on the ground as he bounced along the road. He swung a leg over the animal's back and stuck his head in the door of the smithy.

"The boy at the church said I would find Menno Simons here."

"That's me," said Menno, rising.

"I have a message for you." He handed the priest a sealed letter.

Menno reached in his vest pocket for a coin. "Thank you."

The messenger tipped his hat and crossed over to the inn to tie up his donkey.

Menno broke the seal and looked at the signature. He did not recognize the name.

To Menno Simons, our brother in the faith: I recently met your brother Peter before he joined the Münsterites. He has informed me that you are a priest, with training in Latin and Greek, and that your heart is burning for reforming the church. We are peaceful Anabaptists and do not believe in violence as do the leaders of Münster. We teach our people to live peacefully and to obey their rulers. We are seeking a true reformation of doctrine. When it is safe enough to travel, we would like to meet with you. We have a congregation in Groningen and you are welcome to join us. Your humble servant, Obbe Philips.

Conrad glanced up at him from the floor, where he was reattaching the wheel. "From your brother?" he said hopefully.

"No. Someone who knows him." Menno tucked the letter inside his vest and pulled out a few coins to pay Conrad.

"No charge for the church, Father."

Menno nodded. He thanked the blacksmith and rolled the wheelbarrow back out to the road.

"This Philips follows Melchior's teaching, then, not that of these radicals in Münster," he thought. "Leiden is getting all the attention, but there are others quietly spreading a peaceful doctrine. Why, we're working toward reformation, too, in our own little villages!"

He had not thought of it that way before. The idea quickened his heart.

But he didn't think he was willing to risk visiting Philips in Groningen. Not just yet. Philips would expect him to resign from the Catholic priesthood. And if he was publicly identified as an Anabaptist, his neck might be in danger.

He decided not to reply right away. Perhaps he could find out more about Philips. In the meantime, he had a lot of work to do in Witmarsum.

He clutched at the wheelbarrow handle as it tried to get away from him down the hill.

Fall wore on into winter. The mill owner shut down the mill for the season, and snowflakes covered the still paddles of the wheel in the pond. Menno and Wessel celebrated the Christmas feast with Dirk's family.

Every few weeks Menno had to chase off more missionaries who came from Münster to urge the people to fight for the promised land. Menno's sermons warned against following radicals. He reminded his congregation that they were in a spiritual battle, a battle for their hearts, not their cities and lands.

Menno awoke on a morning in March to the smell of thawing earth. The temperature had risen over night. It felt almost like spring, though he knew they could still get another snowfall before winter was over. He decided to take advantage of the unexpected weather and go for a walk before breakfast.

He laced up his trousers and wriggled into a close-fitting jacket. His hat waited for him by the door.

The birds were out celebrating the warmer air, too. Their songs in the trees boosted his spirits as he followed the road away from the village and through the fields. He decided to pass by the mill pond.

He was startled to hear voices as he neared the pond. "Who would be down here so early?" he wondered.

He rounded a clump of trees, and the bank came into view. Clustered on the edge of the water were a dozen people. They were watching two men out in the cold pond, one being baptized by the other.

One of the men on the bank turned around as Menno approached. He was dressed in baggy, tattered clothes and wore a sword on his hip.

"Peter?" Menno was stunned to recognize his brother. "Peter!" Tears blurred his eyes as he embraced him. "It is good to see you!"

"You are looking well, Menno," said Peter.

"I cannot say the same for you," his brother replied, eyeing the threadbare clothes. "What are you doing here?"

"Using the pond to baptize some new converts."

"But I thought you were still at Münster. I was afraid I'd never see you again."

"We've left Münster," said Peter. He held up his hands in surrender. "Listen, Menno, you were right about Matthijs and Leiden. All they did is bring oppression and sickness to the people. The city is still under siege, and there is talk that Catholics and Protestants are joining together with the bishop's forces to retake the city. We got out while we could."

Menno looked at him hopefully. "And you've come back to Witmarsum?"

"No, we're just passing through," Peter said, shaking his head. "I was hoping to come see you after the baptism. I suppose you won't come with us, but I wanted to try to convince you."

"Come with you where?"

"To Amsterdam!" Peter pointed at one of the two men coming up out of the water. "That's Jan van Geel over there. He's the one that led us out of Münster. He tells us miracles are happening in Amsterdam. There are already five thousand of our people in the city. Soon God will fulfill his promise and establish the New Jerusalem there!"

Menno's jaw dropped. "I can't believe this! Have you not learned your lesson? First you said Strasbourg was the New Jerusalem. Then you said Münster. Now it's Amsterdam?"

"Some say London," said Peter, shrugging, "but there have been no signs and wonders to prove it."

Menno threw his hands in the air. "I don't care if some say it will be in the Americas! They are wrong. They are *all* wrong, Peter! Why can't you see that?"

"Because I have the eyes of faith, faith that can move mountains. You can't see the truth because you are still blinded by the false teaching of the pope." He glared at Menno.

"The pope is wrong, you know I agree with you there. But these men you follow, they are false prophets, too."

"These men are leading us to a new future, Menno. A future

where corruption will be vanquished."

"By the sword?" Menno pointed at his brother's weapon. "Christ said that his kingdom is not of this world. He told his disciple Peter to put away his sword, to turn the other cheek."

"Only for a time. But that time is over now. He has ordained us to usher in a new time!"

"I warned you that your zeal would lead you to violence, and you admit that violence is all you found in Münster. Why do you run headlong into more foolishness?"

Peter's neck was red, but his voice was calm. "I had hoped you would see the light, brother. But it's clear to me that you will not believe. I will have to say good bye." He turned away.

"Peter!"

Peter wouldn't look back. But the group around the pond turned to stare at Menno.

"Are you all as foolish as my brother?" he shouted at them. "Are you so eager to believe anyone who promises you the world? These men will let you die before they admit they have been deceived!"

The group began to move away from the pond, following the road into the woods. Menno watched them go. He felt that he must stop them, but he didn't know how.

"Lord!" he cried. "Change my brother's heart. Take away his foolishness. Increase his knowledge of you. Teach him your way of peace."

He stared down the road long after they had moved out of sight. The joy of the spring weather was gone. The world felt cold to him again. Dejected, he shuffled back to the village.

A week later, the innkeeper's mother took sick. She asked for Menno, and he went to the inn to pray with her.

"Father, teach us to have faith," he prayed aloud. He sat in a chair next to her bed in the darkened room. "No matter what person or sickness opposes us, we trust your wisdom and your goodness—."

A knock sounded, and the door burst open, interrupting his

prayer. Dirk stood in the doorway, out of breath.

"What is so important that you disturb us before the throne of God?" chided Menno.

"Your brother."

Menno felt his heart sink into his belly. He squeezed the woman's hand above her blankets. "Please excuse me, Mother Linck."

He followed Dirk out of the inn and toward the well in the center of the square. "What has happened to my brother?"

"You know the old monastery at Bolsward?" Dirk began, catching his breath.

"Of course. What about it?"

"The Anabaptists seized it on their way to Amsterdam. They were going to stay there for a few days while they gathered men for their cause. But the local rulers sent an army to take it back." Dirk would not look at him. "There was a battle."

Menno sank down on the stone wall that circled the well.

"Are they alright?"

"The army had canons, Father. They stormed the cloister, and all the Anabaptists were executed."

"What about Peter?"

The boy stared at his shoes. "I'm sorry. That is what I'm trying to tell you," he said quietly. "Peter was killed with the others."

The priest shut his eyes. He sat so still that after a few minutes Dirk wondered if he was asleep. But then he opened his eyes again, and Dirk saw the tears shining there.

"Are you sure no one was spared?" he whispered.

"Jan van Geel escaped, but he was the only one. That is all I know."

Menno blinked, forcing back his tears. Across the square, the innkeeper was watching them from his door.

"Go back to the inn and tell Frau Linck I will come to pray with her again tonight," said Menno, rising. "Conrad and Wessel should be told directly about the cloister. The others will find out soon enough. Then go home and get your dinner."

"Will you be all right, Father?"

He nodded. "I am going back to the church," he said, and turned away. Dirk watched him move slowly, head lowered, down the hill toward the church.

Kneeling before the altar, Menno looked up at a wooden cross fastened above it. Light from the window struck it so that it seemed to glow against the dark wall.

"Why am I afraid to risk everything for Christ?" he wondered. "I was afraid to read the Bible. I was afraid to read the banned books of the reformers. I was afraid to leave the priesthood. Yet my misguided brother was willing to give up his life for false prophets!" Tears streamed down his face. "Shouldn't I be willing to risk everything to preach the true gospel of Christ?"

The pulpit Bible was open to the first book of Corinthians, where he had been reading that morning. He got up and went to it. His eyes fell on the words: "No man can lay any foundation other than the one already laid, which is Jesus Christ."

"This movement has conviction," he thought, "but it is built on the wrong foundation. Christ is our only true king. These errant sheep need someone to guide them back to the true path."

He stared up at the cross. "Is that what you would have me do, Lord? Are you calling me to leave the priesthood? Are you calling me to lead these people to repentance and peace?"

He heard movement at the back of the church. Wessel was standing awkwardly in the doorway, both hands on his floppy hat.

"I heard the news," he said quietly. "What can I do, Father?"

Menno went to him. "Pray for me, Wessel," he replied, putting his hands on the tinker's shoulders. "My heart trembles! I've prayed to God with sighs and tears that he would give to me, a sorrowing sinner, the gift of his grace. I ask him to create in me a clean heart. I ask for wisdom and courage to preach his holy Word in purity."

"I ask that for myself also," said Wessel. "I will join you, Menno.

I will follow you as you follow Christ."

Menno gazed beside him at the table full of candles. A few of them had burned out, but the rest burned brightly, their flames climbing higher.

"It may take more sacrifice than we have already made, my friend," Menno said. "But wherever God leads me—whether here in my little country parish, or in the powerful cities of the world—I will not be afraid. We shall build a kingdom of peace on the foundation of Christ!"

In June of 1535, Catholic and Protestant princes joined forces and successfully retook the city of Münster. Jan of Leiden and the other Anabaptist leaders were tortured and executed. The death of his brother in April and the slaughter of the Anabaptists in Münster in June convinced Menno Simons to leave the priesthood and join the Anabaptists as an itinerant preacher of peace. In 1537, he was ordained by Obbe Philips and became the leader of the non-violent Dutch Anabaptist movement. His followers became known as Mennonites.

He wrote several books, including his most famous work, The Foundation of the Christian Doctrine. *He married a woman named Gertrude and had three children. His family was constantly on the run from the law, as Anabaptists continued to be persecuted after the fall of Münster. But he was never captured. He died after a long illness on January 31, 1561.*

J⊕HN CALVIN: T⊕ TAKE A WIFE

JULY 1538. THE FREE REPUBLIC OF STRASBOURG
(NOW PART OF FRANCE).

THE HOME OF Martin and Elisabeth Bucer stood on a narrow street. It was a two-story house with open shutters at the windows and a few vines creeping up the stone. A single broad step led up to the wooden door.

The young preacher stood in the street across from the house and wiped his brow with a clean, neatly-folded handkerchief. It was July, and he had worked up a sweat following the directions to the house. Tucking the handkerchief into his pocket, he picked up his bag, climbed the stoop to the door, and knocked sharply three times.

"Good evening, Monsieur," he said to the man who answered. "I received a letter from you. My name is——."

"John Calvin!" cried Martin Bucer, taking his hand in a crushing grip. "I know who you are. Welcome, welcome!"

Martin appeared to be nearly twenty years older than his visitor. He had a square jaw with deep laugh lines and a rather prominent nose.

He threw open the door. Two little girls peeked out from behind his legs. "Do not be rude, children," he said, pushing them forward. "Say hello to Monsieur Calvin. He is a famous scholar!"

"Hello, Monsieur," they said, shyly looking at the floor.

"Go find your brothers and run off to the kitchen," Martin said. He took John by the arm and pulled him toward the door. "Come in, my friend. You are just in time for dinner."

John stepped inside. He immediately noticed two things.

The first was that it was a comfortable house. He was standing in a narrow reception room with an open fireplace at the far end and a curved staircase that led up to the second floor. A row of windows facing the street were hung with draperies, and candleholders decorated the walls.

The second thing he noticed was the aroma of fresh bread and roasted meat. His stomach growled.

"Elisabeth!" Martin bellowed. "He's here!"

A woman came through the doorway beyond the staircase, tucking a strand of hair into her bonnet. Her face radiated warmth. "Monsieur Calvin? What a pleasure to meet you."

Martin held out his arm, and she slipped her hand through the crook at his elbow. "My wife, Elisabeth," said Martin proudly.

John gave her a formal bow and she laughed.

"A young man with manners! I welcome such a guest any day." She glanced at her husband with a look of mischief. "All Martin has said to me for days is 'Calvin is coming, Calvin is coming.' It is good to see you. I was beginning to think you were a figment of his imagination!"

"I hope the dinner I smell isn't a figment of my imagination," retorted Martin.

She chuckled again. "You smell the goose the children are eating right now. But don't worry, there is a second one roasting on the spit for us." She turned back to their guest. "You will join us, won't you, Monsieur Calvin?"

"With gratitude, Madame."

"Then I'll let Anne know we are ready for dinner."

She went back through the doorway, and Martin pointed to a low table under one of the front windows. "Leave your things here and come with me."

John tucked his bag in the corner, and took care to place his cap on the table precisely opposite the oil lamp.

Beyond the doorway, the next room held a large dining table surrounded by straight-backed chairs. Candles flickered on the sideboard. Elisabeth joined them there.

"Normally our table is full," said Martin, pulling out a chair for his guest. "But my boarding students all seem to have found other places to be tonight. So we get you to ourselves!"

Anne, the kitchen maid, came in and set a trencher of soup in front of each of them.

Martin raised his hands over the table. "Praise be to God for supplying all of our needs, including this food. Amen!"

He picked up his bowl in both hands and sipped straight from it. "What a privilege to have the author of the *Institutes* here in our city!" he declared.

"You see what I mean?" said Elisabeth, smiling across the table at John. "Now tell us, Monsieur, you have come from Geneva?"

"Yes. I have been there for the last eighteen months."

"It is so beautiful there on the lake in the mountains."

John frowned. "Beautiful, yes, but the state of the church is most distressing. I consider my exile from Geneva a sign from God that I am free from that city!"

"Really?" She passed him the salt cellar. "Why did you go there?"

"I was actually on my way here, to Strasbourg," he explained. "I had to take a detour because of the war between King Francis and Emperor Charles, and intended to stay in Geneva only one night. But Farel—do you know Guillaume Farel?"

Martin chuckled. "Big man, wild eyes, fiery red beard! Yes, I know Farel."

"Well, Farel came and found me at the inn and told me about Geneva's troubles. He demanded that I stay to help him. He said God would curse my studies if I didn't!"

"He can be very persuasive," agreed Martin. "So that's how you got involved in the city government?"

John nodded. "We gave the people a confession of faith, which united them as a city. And we set up strict laws to help them keep it. We even had to kick out John Stordeur and other Anabaptists who would not submit to these laws and were trying to preach a different doctrine. But then the province of Bern—our political ally—took over Geneva. They began to insist on making decisions for the church that only ministers should make, like how often we serve communion and which church members we can discipline."

He shook his head with disappointment. "Farel and I were not about to give up the reforms we had put into place, so we refused their restrictions. The city council expelled us."

"Where did Farel go?" asked Elisabeth.

"To Neuchâtel."

"And you answered my invitation to come here," said Martin. "Well, Geneva's loss is Strasbourg's gain! We have many French Reformed refugees here who have fled persecution. They are desperate for a pastor. God's timing could not have been better."

"He is sovereign over all," John agreed. "I submit to his call here."

"You are a good man," Martin declared. "Elisabeth and I will be happy to give you a place to stay until you are settled here. We have many heads to shelter, but this is a big house. As long as you don't mind a little noise, you will be happy enough here. Plus, I have a bit of a library that a studious man like yourself will appreciate."

"I see why your home is known as the 'inn of righteousness' around here. I will be thankful for the food and company."

"Excellent!" Martin reached across the table to shake his hand. "I will show you to the church tomorrow morning. The congregation is anxious to meet you."

"They have the most beautiful singing voices," Elisabeth said. "You'll love worshipping with them."

The kitchen girl came in and presented them with a platter of goose.

"Absolutely lovely, Anne!" declared Martin, digging in.

Elisabeth waited until John had taken a few bites. "Forgive my curiosity, Monsieur," she said. "But how did you come to the Reformed faith?"

John cleared his throat. "I was exposed to Luther's teachings while I was studying law at the University of Orleans. After I began to study his writings, God changed my heart and mind. By the time I returned to Paris to teach law, Luther's followers were being persecuted. I was forced into hiding here and there until I finally went to Basel, and from there to Geneva."

"And that is where you published the *Institutes?*" jumped in Martin.

"In Basel, yes. I wanted to produce an introduction manual to our faith."

They waited for him to go on, but he shifted in his chair. "I have talked far too much about myself," he declared. "What about you, Martin? You have been a leader of the Reformed church in Strasbourg for some time. How were you converted?"

"By Martin Luther, in the flesh," declared Martin. "I used to be a Dominican monk, you know. But I was present at the Heidelberg Disputation in 1518 where Luther defended his teachings. Say what you will about that man, he is a passionate preacher!"

"And you, Madame?"

"I left the convent to marry this reformer!"

John's eyebrows shot up at Martin. "Why, Luther married a nun, too. You really do follow him!"

Martin grinned. "Ah, except I did it first. In this case, Luther follows me!"

After dinner, Elisabeth showed John to one of the six small bedrooms on the second floor and reminded him he was welcome to stay as long as necessary.

He spent the rest of the week meeting people at the Bucer's dinner table and preparing his first sermon for Strasbourg.

On Sunday, he arose at dawn, put on his black academic robe, and walked to the church with Martin and Elisabeth. He was surprised to see a crowd already waiting for him.

"I told you they were eager to meet you!" declared Martin.

The new French preacher climbed the staircase into the circular pulpit and looked out over the congregation. "We must remember that wherever we go, the cross of Jesus Christ will follow us," he told them. "Though we are refugees in Strasbourg, we have a heavenly home waiting for us. Even when our lives seem disrupted, God in his providence has a plan for us. He has a reason for everything."

They lifted their voices together to sing psalms in French. Tears welled in his eyes as he listened to them sing, and he squeezed them shut before anyone could see. He preferred to keep his emotions to himself. But inwardly he prayed, "Eternal Father, I praise you for such sweet fellowship with your people. Thank you for calling me to another congregation where I may serve you."

He was soon busy with the work of the church in Strasbourg. He preached several times a week. He taught Bible studies. He visited his congregation in their homes. He answered the letters that came in from church leaders across Europe.

Eventually, he found a house to rent and hired a housekeeper. But compared to the hustle and bustle of the Bucer house, his was quiet and empty. So he often found himself around Martin and Elisabeth's table, talking about the Bible.

"What do you think, Martin?" asked Elisabeth one night. "Do you think John comes here for your conversation or my biscuits?"

"I'm certain it is for your conversation," replied Martin. "I am not nearly as witty as you."

John allowed himself a smile. "I come here to watch your conversations with each other," he admitted. "I've never seen such a fine marriage."

His hosts looked at each other with a knowing smile. "Someone is thinking of getting married," said Martin.

John blushed and raised his hand in objection. "No, I'm not. Marriage is a distraction."

"Marriage is a blessing, John," Elisabeth corrected.

"You should get married," said Martin. "Marriage is good for a minister of the gospel. It brings life to the home."

"I have a plan to bring life to my home already," he insisted. "I'm going to take in some students who want to become pastors. They will receive training, and it will help me pay the rent."

John made it known that he was looking for students, and in a few weeks several young men were renting rooms in his house. He held theology classes with them and put them to work helping him with his church duties. He gave them books to read, dictated letters to them, and put them in charge of prayer meetings.

Running a household of students was hard work. John's housekeeper did all the cooking and cleaning—and all the complaining. He wanted to dismiss her for being so unpleasant, but he needed her help. Between his church duties, his students, and his writing, he barely had time to pay the bills.

And his congregation was growing. The persecution of Reformed Christians in France was spreading, and they were fleeing to cities that would allow them to worship freely. Every week, more refugees arrived in Strasbourg. They were eager to hear the preaching of the famous scholar.

One evening, a knock came at his door. The housekeeper was already gone for the day. John had sent his students out to visit with church members so he could spend a few hours writing in peace. He really didn't want to receive any visitors tonight, but the knocking continued.

Sighing, he set down his pen and went through the front room to the door. A man and woman stood on his doorstep.

"You?" said John in surprise. "What are you doing here?"

"You kicked me out of Geneva, remember?"

"Monsieur Stordeur——."

"And my wife, Idelette de Bure," said Stordeur, drawing her forward.

"It is an honor to meet you, Monsieur Calvin," she said. She was a slight woman with fair skin, dark hair, and thin eyebrows. John could tell from her ruffled collar and carefully-polished shoes that she considered this an important visit.

"Madame," he acknowledged with a stiff bow.

He turned back to her husband. "I can't kick you out of Strasbourg, Stordeur, but I'm not going to debate with you about baptism again. Good day." He began to shut the door.

Stordeur shoved his foot in the door and winced. "I'm not here to debate," he insisted. "A friend let me borrow a copy of your *Institutes* and I have considered your teachings. I am here to learn from you."

John eyed him suspiciously.

"Please, Monsieur," said Idelette. "My husband speaks highly of you. He is telling the truth."

He frowned, but slowly opened the door. "Very well then," he said. "Come in. I don't mean to be rude."

He led them into his sitting room, where a modest fire crackled in the grate. There were few furnishings, but a large desk was stacked neatly with books and papers. He waved them to the only two comfortable seats and drew up his desk chair.

"So, you have come to Strasbourg," he said. "Persecution, I assume?"

Stordeur nodded. "Yes. The Anabaptists in Liege have become a target. We had to leave."

"I suppose you brought a few friends with you?"

Stordeur laughed at John's dour expression. "Only a few, Calvin. But I promise you, we will not cause trouble here. We are happy to be alive with our families in the free city of Strasbourg."

"You have children?"

"We have two," answered Idelette, with a mother's pride. "A son and a daughter."

"Exile is difficult," John admitted. "I'm sure it is even more so when you have children to look after."

"That is why God blesses us with faithful companions," said Stordeur, with a smiling glance at his wife. He leaned forward in his seat. "Calvin, we are interested in your doctrine. Will you allow me to bring my family to your church?"

John considered the question. "I will not turn you away from the worship of our God, as long as you respect our teachings," he said finally.

"That is fair," agreed Stordeur. "Now, my wife and I have some questions about those teachings. Do you mind explaining a few things to us tonight?"

John glanced at the stack of papers waiting on his desk and sighed. "My work will be there tomorrow," he reminded himself. "Apparently God has sent the Stordeurs to me for a reason."

"All right," he said, leaning back and folding his hands across his lap. "What do you wish to learn?"

He spent the next several hours teaching them the Scriptures. They seemed genuinely grateful when they left, and invited him to have dinner with them later in the week.

The following day, he told Martin and Elisabeth about the unexpected visit. They were in their usual seats around the Bucer dinner table.

"It sounds like you underestimated Monsieur Stordeur," said Martin. "When he said that he wanted to have an open conversation about baptism and other doctrines, he meant it."

"So it appears," said Calvin.

"I must go visit his wife and welcome her," said Elisabeth. "What is she like?"

He thought for a moment. "Quiet, but strong, I think. Like you, a good conversationalist. They seem happy."

She beamed at him.

"You *are* thinking of marriage!" declared Martin.

"Maybe I am," John said, shrugging. "I cannot run the house alone. I have never been good at managing my expenses, and there is so much work to be done."

"A fine marriage is about having the right companion," said Martin. "It is more than cooking and sewing and taking the children to the shoemaker."

Elisabeth laughed. "If I could just get Martin to do one of those! But he is right. You need a spiritual companion."

"Yes, someone to share the burdens of your ministry," insisted Martin. "It is not good for a man to be alone. And marriage is a living sermon of the believer's union with Christ."

"I would not know how to find a wife."

"That is what friends are for," Martin explained. "Those who know you best can help you find the right woman. I know several beautiful French ladies of marrying age."

John shook his head. "I am not looking for a beautiful woman."

"You are looking for an ugly woman?"

"No, no." The color rose in John's cheeks. "What I mean is that I am not like the Greeks who attacked Troy just to take a wife! I do not intend to marry for beauty alone. Beauty is not disagreeable, but it will not move me to marry a woman."

Martin smacked his thigh. "Ah, beauty is not disagreeable, he says!"

Elisabeth ignored her husband's guffaw. "John, I have never met a young man who has such control of his feelings! Tell me, what *are* the qualifications of a wife of Monsieur John Calvin?"

"Pious," he said. "Modest. Economical. Patient. Concerned for my health." He ticked off each quality on his fingers as he said it.

"Is that all?" Martin was biting his lip to keep from grinning.

John looked at him earnestly. "Will you help me find such a woman?"

"Let me think about that." Martin leaned toward him and scrutinized his face. "Are you keeping that beard?"

"My beard?" John looked startled, and put a hand to his goatee. "Well, yes, I was thinking of growing it longer."

"In that case, I hope the young ladies have fewer demands for a husband than you have for a wife!" Martin slapped him on the back and laughed again.

Elisabeth reached across the table and patted John's arm. "Of course we'll help you. We'll be celebrating your marriage before you know it!"

John went into his sitting room late that night and lit a candle at his desk. He owed Farel a letter anyway, and now it felt urgent to contact him. He dipped his pen in the ink bottle and began to write:

Health to you, my excellent brother, Farel. It is good to write you again. I have decided to seek a wife, and I ask my friends to help. If you find a godly woman, please let me know. Would you plan to come here at Easter, so you can officiate at my wedding? Martin Bucer sends his salutations. May the Lord preserve you in all safety for the good of the church. Yours, John Calvin.

He refused to let himself dwell on the search for a wife, content that his friends would find the right woman soon. Instead, he threw himself even more into his duties at church and with his students. He began to revise his famous book and took notes for another one he wanted to write. He traveled to meetings with other reformers in nearby cities. And his congregation kept growing. The Stordeur family even joined the church.

One night at the Bucer's table, Martin introduced him to a young man.

"Philip has been telling me about his sister," said Martin, as they passed a loaf of bread around the table. "I think she might be a good match for you, John."

John stopped chewing and took a closer look at the young man. "Do I know her?"

"No," said Philip. "But we're German, and we know many of Luther's friends. They will recommend her to you if you should wish to contact them."

"And I have met her several times myself," Martin agreed. "You would like her."

"I see," said John. "I suppose I should arrange to meet her."

Philip cleared his throat. "I hope you don't mind, but I've already spoken to my family about you. I am prepared to discuss the terms of her dowry." He pulled out a letter from the pocket inside his coat and slid it across the table.

John balanced his piece of bread carefully on the edge of his plate and brushed the crumbs from his fingers. He had not expected to face such a decision tonight.

"Well, take a look!" urged Martin. "She is a wealthy woman and quite interested in supporting your scholarship."

John unfolded the letter and read it quickly. He couldn't believe the amount of money offered in the arrangement! "This is too much," he said, pushing the paper back across the table.

"Too much?" said Philip. "I don't understand."

Elisabeth set down her mug. "I've never heard a man quibble about too *much* money."

"She is too wealthy," John explained. "I'm a writer and a pastor. A rich woman will not be content with such a life."

Martin leaned on the table. "John, you gave us a long list of qualifications. You said the right woman would be modest, pious, patient, good with money. This woman is all of these things."

John shook his head. "Her fortune is above my condition. I'm afraid she'll remember her education and wealth too often and regret her decision to marry me."

Candles flickered in the silence.

"My sister is a godly woman," insisted Philip. "She keeps her commitments."

The three of them looked at him expectantly. He suddenly felt surrounded.

"Does she speak French?" he asked.

Philip looked confused. "She is German."

"But is she willing to learn French?"

"I don't think that was in the job description you gave us," Martin reminded him.

John felt a surge of relief. "How can a marriage work if the husband and wife speak different languages?" He looked Philip in the eye. "I have the highest respect for your sister, Monsieur, and I thank you for your generous offer. But I am certain there is someone else out there for me. I will wait patiently on God's providence."

So John waited on God for several months. He was soon forced to write to Farel and tell him to cancel his Easter wedding plans.

From time to time, Elisabeth asked John how his search was going.

"My former colleague Farel wrote to me about a woman he knows," reported John one night at dinner.

"That's wonderful!" Elisabeth said. She smiled and leaned across the table. "Does she speak French?"

He laughed at her. "Yes, she speaks French. And she is a firm supporter of Reformed doctrine. But——." He paused.

"But what? She is too rich?"

"No, she has modest means. But she is fifteen years older than I am. It is too great an age difference."

"Oh, John. You are so particular!" She threw up her hands in exasperation.

"I see no reason to rush marriage," he said firmly. "If God ordains that I marry, he will bring the right woman at the right time."

But he was beginning to think he was not meant to marry.

"You are here so often we might as well give you back your room upstairs!" Martin said one night, opening the door to John.

John smiled, but his eyes were troubled.

"What is on your mind tonight, Pastor?" Martin asked, as he waited for John to hang up his coat.

John sighed. "I have been content to serve the church here. But I wonder if God is leading me to move on."

"Move on? What do you mean?"

"The city of Geneva has been in disarray. The magistrates that supported Farel and I are now opposing the government of Bern."

Martin raised his eyebrows. "You are thinking of returning to Geneva?"

"They have asked me to," he admitted. "I said no. But I'm certain they will not accept that answer."

Martin opened his mouth to object, but an urgent pounding on the door stopped him. He threw open the door.

A white-faced boy stared at them. "Master Bucer! Master Calvin! Some of the townspeople are very ill. It happened so quickly!"

The two reformers looked at one another in dismay.

"Plague," John declared.

"Elisabeth!" Martin shouted. He ran to find his cloak and cap. "The last plague killed three of my students in only a few days, John."

John jerked his coat off the hook where he had just hung it. "I need to check on my congregation."

They rushed out the door.

Within a day, panic struck the city. Calvin went from house to house in the French neighborhood, checking on members of his church. When he arrived at the Stordeur home, he was dismayed to see their little girl answer the door.

"Are your parents ill, Judith?"

She nodded and pointed toward the back of the house.

John ran into the darkened bedroom and found Idelette bathing her husband's face with a wet rag. Stordeur shivered in his bed, delirious.

"He's burning up," she said tearfully. "Nothing seems to help."

John was moved with compassion for his former opponent. "Let us pray for him," he said, kneeling beside her.

"You have done all you can, Madame," he said quietly, after they had prayed together. "I have to check on the others. But I'll come back tomorrow."

She nodded. "Thank you, Pastor."

At the door, he crouched down next to Judith and put a hand on her shoulder. "Get your mother something to drink and eat," he said, "and then find your brother and go to the neighbors until your mother comes for you. Do you understand?"

The little girl looked just like her mother as she bravely wiped a tear from her face and nodded.

By the time John returned the next day, Stordeur was dead.

John sent Idelette and her children to stay with friends in another part of the city. Over the next few weeks, several more members of his congregation were lost to the plague. But eventually, people stopped getting sick. Some who had fled returned to their homes. It seemed the plague was over.

"Sometimes God deals harshly with us for our sin," Calvin declared from his pulpit one Sunday morning. "Sometimes he brings trials to make us stronger, and sometimes to make us repent of our sin. God blesses us as a city, and tries us as a city. We must, therefore, repent as a city."

The congregation was smaller than usual. They were huddled together in the middle of the church. His eyes met the face of Idelette, sitting with her two children. The space next to them on the bench was empty.

His voice softened. "But when God brings pain our way,

sometimes—like Job—we can find solace in the blessings to come."

The psalm singing refreshed him, but he was tired after church. Martin and Elisabeth insisted that he come back to their house and have something to eat.

Anne had left smoked cheese and bread on the sideboard. Elisabeth fixed plates for the children and fed them in the kitchen, then joined Martin and John in the dining room.

"Your housekeeper is not feeding you well," she said to John.

He groaned. "Do not speak of that woman on the Lord's Day!"

"Is that a joke?" said Martin. "I'm shocked to find you with a sense of humor!"

John ignored the taunt.

"Elisabeth is right, John. You are not looking well. You cannot keep up your preaching if you become ill. Let your students handle the visitations this week so you can rest."

"Perhaps I will," John agreed.

Elisabeth set a plate in front of him. "I visited Idelette de Bure yesterday."

"How is she?" asked Martin.

She sat down at the table. "It is difficult to be a young widow. Her faith is strong. She blesses God for the health of her children. And I think her family has some money, so she has not had to depend on charity. But she is lonely."

She looked meaningfully at Martin.

His eyes lit up. "That's it, John!" he exclaimed.

"That's what?"

"The end of your quest for a wife. Why don't you marry Idelette? She has every quality you are looking for, does she not? And she seems to have great respect for you."

John considered that for a few moments. He could think of no objections. In fact, it seemed quite reasonable.

"Well?" said Elisabeth.

John's face was grave. "Do you think she would have me?"

Martin slapped his hand down on the table. "You'll have to ask her and find out!" he cried. He was so excited, he grabbed his wife's hand and kissed it, right there in front of his fellow pastor.

John smiled all through dinner.

The next day, in his formal way, John put on his cap and his black robe and went to Idelette's house.

"Pastor Calvin," she said when she answered the door. "Would you like to come in?"

"No, no," he stammered. "I have come to ask you a question." He twisted his cap between his hands.

"Yes?"

"I am looking for a wife," he finally said.

"Oh." Her eyes grew wide. "Oh!"

His face reddened, but he continued with his speech. "Idelette de Bure, would you consent to marry me? I am not a rich man, and the life of a pastor and a scholar is not easy. I have a household of students and a sharp-tongued housekeeper. But I will be your faithful companion before God."

"Well, Monsieur Calvin," she said after a moment. "I am not the youngest bride, and I have two children. But I dare say I could do something about that housekeeper. And it would be an honor to become the wife of the man who taught me the Reformed faith." She smiled at him. "Yes, I will marry you."

His breath caught, but he willed himself to go on. "Thank you. Er, I am pleased to hear it. I mean, I shall ask Monsieur Farel to come to Strasbourg as soon as possible to marry us. And I shall ask Madame Bucer to come see you and make the arrangements."

"All right," she said, still smiling.

He turned away from the door, afraid his satisfaction would show on his face, and walked as fast as he could to the Bucer's.

"She said yes," he blurted out when Martin opened the door.

Martin grinned and yanked him inside.

"I don't believe it!" he shouted. "John Calvin is getting married!"

The whole household came running then. The youngest children began to dance around them. Elisabeth congratulated him with a warm handshake.

"You were right all along, John," she said. "Our sovereign God was preparing just the right woman for you. All you had to do was wait on his providence!"

John and Idelette were married in August 1540. A few months later, Calvin and Farel agreed to return to Geneva and reorganize the church government there. Idelette gave birth to three more children, but they all died as infants. In 1549, just nine years after they were married, Idelette died. John called her "the best companion of my life" and never remarried. John published numerous revisions of his Institutes of the Christian Religion—*considered one of the most important Reformed treatises ever written—and commentaries on almost every book of the Bible. He led the Reformation in Geneva for nearly twenty-five years, becoming a citizen just five years before his death in 1564. He was buried according to his wishes in an unmarked grave.*

Big Changes in the Reformation World

THE CHURCH WAS not the only aspect of life that was changing in the sixteenth and seventeenth centuries. Other changes were happening in society, in art and culture, and in science. These changes had a big impact on the way people of the Reformation era understood their world.

CHANGES IN SOCIETY

Life in Medieval Europe was organized around a system that classified people into four categories: clergy, royalty, nobility, and workers. Though each group of people had duties to the other, they did not have the same rights and privileges. The pope ruled the church, while the emperor ruled the kings. Kings granted noblemen *fiefs* or lands that came with certain obligations. The noble who received a fief was the king's *vassal* and was required to supply military support and taxes to the king. In turn, the king would protect the vassal's rights and knight his sons. The land was farmed by the *serfs* or working class. Serfs were not slaves, but they were bound to live on and work the vassal's land. This system was called the *feudal system* (from the word "fief").

The feudal system survived for centuries. But by the time of the Renaissance it was fading. This was partly because of peasant revolts, and also because of the rise of a merchant class that began to support itself apart from farming. In England, serfdom ended in the mid sixteenth century. But it lasted in France until 1789 and in Russia until 1861.

CHANGES IN ART AND CULTURE

During the Renaissance, scholars became especially interested in subjects related to mankind. They studied history, read ancient books, and explored the human ability to reason.

Poets and other writers looked to the ancient texts and myths for inspiration. One of the most famous was the English actor William Shakespeare (1564-1616), who wrote many plays including *A Midsummer Night's Dream*, *Julius Caesar*, and *Hamlet*.

The artists of the Renaissance also showed more interest in painting and sculpting the human body. Michelangelo (1475-1564) painted detailed scenes on the ceiling of the Sistine Chapel, including *The Creation of Adam*. Leonardo da Vinci (1452-1519) was also interested in scientific experiments and botany.

Art was controversial during the Reformation. Some reformers believed that *icons* (art depicting biblical figures and saints) displayed in church were forms of idolatry, so they destroyed them. Luther considered art a useful teaching tool and did not dismiss it. Some portraits we now have of the reformers were painted by famous artists of the period, like Lucas Cranach the Elder (1472-1553).

CHANGES IN SCIENCE

Along with a new era in Christian doctrine came a new era in science, called the *Copernican Revolution*. For centuries, astronomers had held the view of Ptolemy (ca. 100-170), a philosopher, astronomer, and mathematician of ancient Alexandria. Ptolemy believed that the sun, moon, planets, and stars revolved around the earth. But in 1543, Nicolaus Copernicus published a book titled *On the Revolutions of Heavenly Bodies*. Copernicus (without the benefit of a telescope, which was not invented until 1605) said that planets revolve around the sun, not the other way around.

Astronomer Tycho Brahe (1546-1601) attempted to combine the two views, claiming that the sun revolves around the earth, but all other planets revolve around the sun. Brahe's student Johannes Kepler (1571-1630) did accept Copernicus' view and even made corrections to it. By observing the planet Mars, he discovered that the orbit of a planet is not circular, as Copernicus thought, but elliptical, like an oval.

But in 1616, Catholic leaders decided that the Copernican view was contrary to the views of the ancient church fathers. So when Galileo Galilei (1564-1642) attempted to prove the Copernican view in his book *Dialogue Concerning the Two Chief World Systems* in 1632, his books were condemned by the Inquisition. He was placed under house arrest for the rest of his life for challenging the authority of the church. But later astronomers would prove that Copernicus and Galileo were right.

Galileo's theory of gravity influenced Sir Isaac Newton (1643-1727), who wrote a book called *Mathematical Principles of Natural Philosophy*. Among his many accomplishments, Newton discovered calculus and analyzed light through a prism.

With the changing structure of society, advances in art and science, and the reformers' calls to transform church government and doctrine, everyday life in the Reformation world was changing rapidly. It was both a frightening and exciting time to live.

KATHERINE PARR: FOR SUCH A TIME AS THIS

JUNE 1546. THE COURT OF HENRY VIII OF ENGLAND.

THE KING'S COURT was quiet at this late hour. A woman hurried through the shadowy corridors, her full crimson skirts rustling against chairs and door handles. Rounding a corner quickly, her plumed cap shifted in front of her eyes. She shoved it back over her bundle of brown hair and kept moving.

"Be careful, my queen," whispered one of the young ladies behind her, snatching at the heavily-embroidered hem. "Your dress is stirring up dust."

"That hardly matters, Agnes," the queen whispered back, barely turning her head.

"But you're walking too fast! You'll draw attention to yourself."

The queen waved a careless hand. "I must see Anne immediately."

"Can't you leave that duty to someone else, Katherine?" hissed another woman, straining to keep up with them. "You don't want to get involved in this mess."

The queen stopped suddenly and spun around to face them. "Anne is a friend, Margaret!" she whispered sharply, glaring at her ladies-in-waiting. Her concerned face glowed pale in the dim light of the candles along the wall. "As queen, I may be the only one who can save her life."

The young women hung their heads and nodded. When the queen hurried on again, they ran to catch up with her. But as the three of them turned into a stairwell, a man rushed out and threw up his hands to stop them.

"Dr. Wendy!" chided Agnes. "You nearly scared us to death!"

"Good thing we didn't scream," said Margaret, "or the guards might have shot you believing the queen to be in danger. Have you lost your senses?"

"I have not," insisted the doctor. "I was informed of your plan to help Anne, and I am here to keep you from making a grave mistake."

"Saving a woman's life is never a mistake, Doctor!" cried the queen. She stepped around him, but Dr. Wendy put out his hand in front of her again.

"There is more at stake here than one woman's life, my queen," he said. "We shouldn't talk here."

"He's right," urged Agnes, her lace cap bobbing.

"We're all just concerned for your safety," agreed Margaret.

"It's Anne that is in danger, not me," declared Katherine. "I am the king's wife!"

The two ladies-in-waiting stiffened and looked at one another in alarm.

Dr. Wendy lowered his voice. "You're Henry's sixth wife," he said carefully, "and I dare not remind you what happened to some of your predecessors."

At that, the queen's steady gaze faltered. She allowed the doctor to guide her out of the corridor. Agnes and Margaret followed them in silence back to the queen's suite.

In the safety of her sitting room, the queen felt bolder again. She had sent her ladies away and was now alone with the doctor. A plate of oranges sat on the table between them, untouched.

"Anne Askew is my friend," said Katherine, leaning forward on the edge of her chair. "She is only twenty-three years old. What harm could she possibly do to King Henry or the Lord Chancellor Wriothesley?"

"The Reformed teachings are illegal."

"So is torturing a noble! Don't you know what they do to people in the Tower of London?"

Dr. Wendy appealed to her with sad eyes. "Anne has chosen her path. Do not let her pain be in vain."

"I don't want her to be in pain at all!"

"She is strong. I am told that she refuses to identify any other Reformed sympathizers."

The queen received this information in silence.

"Don't you see, Katherine? Anne is protecting you. She cannot influence the king, but you can."

She looked away.

"You have the closest relationship with the king, and therefore a great responsibility," pleaded the doctor. "It is no secret that his health is poor. When he is gone, the Reformed must be prepared to bring the truth to the Church of England."

Her delicate chin trembled. "What will they do with Anne?" she asked quietly.

He reached forward and took her hand. "Anne's fate is sealed, Katherine. You don't want to know the details. But you have already made great strides in making Henry more sympathetic to Reformed doctrines. There is much more to do. He listens to you."

"I do not know for how much longer he will listen to my words," insisted Katherine, shaking her head. "I am not his doctor of theology. I am his wife. When he is sick and in pain, he has even less patience with me."

"You have been called to this task." Dr. Wendy's voice became irritated. "When will you embrace it?"

She threw herself off the couch and faced him. "You have a short memory, Doctor! Did you not just remind me how some of Henry's past wives lost their heads when they lost his favor?"

He stood, too, his voice rising. "I believe you are here for a purpose, Katherine. Think about it. You grew up in the court. You were engaged to Sir Thomas Seymour until the king broke it off and married you himself. Any number of scenarios could have happened, but they didn't. You became queen instead."

"What is your point, Dr. Wendy?"

He looked at her earnestly. "Perhaps you are here for such a time as this."

She turned away and went to the fireplace. The chambermaid had banked the fire hours ago, but coals still glowed under the ashes. She thought of Anne. How easily her life could be snuffed out, just like the flames that had warmed the room earlier.

The doctor picked up his hat and went to stand behind her. His voice was steady. "You want to help Anne? Help her by accepting her sacrifice and making it count."

Without turning, she said, "I'm not the shrewd politician you think I am."

"Yes, my queen, you are. You just need to believe it, as I do."

He left her staring at the coals in the grate.

Late the next morning, Katherine met the king in his garden for their daily walk. She was more pale than usual and had dark circles under her eyes, but Henry was in too much pain to notice.

They set out on the gravel paths, passing by trimmed hedges and ivy-planted urns. The sky was overcast, but the day was warm. Henry was sweating and limping heavily.

"If he lost weight," Katherine thought, "his leg wouldn't hurt nearly as much." But she knew that because the pain was so intense, he could no longer get out and hunt or play sports as before.

He sensed the direction of her thoughts. "There was a day," he said, straightening his massive shoulders, "when I could take the King of France head on in a wrestling match! Now, my leg is doing to me what many archers in battle have failed to do—it's killing me."

She gave him her arm, and he leaned against her. She was conscious of just how small she was compared to him. Most men were taller than she was, and Henry was considerably taller than most men.

"I and my ladies continue to pray for your healing," she said. "Prince Edward, Princesses Mary and Elizabeth, even Archbishop Cranmer—we all pray for you."

"God listens to my archbishop more than he listens to the pope, I think!" said Henry, grinning despite the pain. He clamped an affectionate hand over hers. "And as for my children, I am pleased that they accept you as a mother. Elizabeth tells me that you constantly remind her to follow Christ."

She shrugged and smiled. "They are my family now."

He nodded his approval. "Well, what were we discussing yesterday in our walk?"

"Last we talked—." She paused as if she was trying to remember, but she already knew what she wanted to say. "I believe I wondered what you thought about giving more freedom to the Reformed. We have already broken off our relationship with Rome. So I wondered, in your wisdom and experience, what would keep us from showing the world just how tolerant we could be."

Henry laughed. It was a deep, resonant sound. "We cannot because we have laws, my dear Kate."

"Yes, but surely, with your unlimited power, you could change those laws," reminded Katherine. "Has not God given you such rights?"

"Of course." He squinted at her, his eyes slits in his fleshy face. "Do you question the teachings of the church?"

"You have already revealed to the English people the abuses of the Roman church. I only wonder what other errors they may have committed."

He didn't reply.

"Both you and I have known some of those who turned out to be Reformed, and they were good people in every way, meaning no harm."

"I wish I could say that was true, Kate," he sighed. "But you give them too much credit. What they propose is treasonous, and if I weren't here to stop them, they would corrupt the English church."

She pressed on. "But surely——."

Henry stumbled on the gravel path. He managed to right himself, but not before twisting his already throbbing leg. Katherine reached out, but he shrugged off her hands.

"I am not a child that I should require the assistance of a woman!" he chided.

She backed away. "Forgive me, my husband. I meant no disrespect."

He grunted and rubbed at his knee. Sweat dripped from his chin. He began to hobble slowly forward again, wincing with each step. "You didn't finish your sentence," he said irritably. "Were we not having a conversation?"

"Of course, Henry." She came alongside him again without touching him. "I was simply remarking that surely their actions are treasonous only because you have declared it to be treason. But by right, if you should decide that their teachings are not heresy, you could reverse that charge."

"Do you believe their teachings are true?" he demanded.

"I am not your teacher," she said carefully, avoiding his gaze, "but you know that some of our best English professors are favorable to Reformed ideas."

"They should approach me about it instead of sending the queen in their place."

"Oh, I raise these questions only from my own curiosity." She gave him a weak smile. "I know some of them have come to you about these things. But you must admit it is not easy for them. Who is not intimidated by the king?"

"Not you, apparently." He shot her a look. "What is it, Kate, that you believe needs to be changed?"

She hesitated.

"In every conversation," the king continued, "you take it upon yourself to show me from Scripture why you think I should consider further changes to the church. You have made your argument for removing the so-called idols of Rome from our worship and their rituals from our services. You have even attempted to prove to me why you think there is merit in the teachings of the Reformed. Should I suspect you of being one of them?"

She pulled away from him slightly and swallowed hard. "Of course not, my dear Henry. It's just that I so enjoy our discussions…"

She was interrupted again when his leg stiffened suddenly and he reached out for the hedge to steady himself. She tried to take his arm, but this time he pushed her hand away fiercely. "I said, I do not need your help!"

"I'm sorry," she whispered. "It is my instinct. I just hate to see someone I love so dearly in so much pain."

He hobbled to a bench near the fountain at the center of the garden and sank down heavily. When she remained where she was, he gestured to her to come. She sat on the edge of the bench with her hands in her lap.

"Why have we not had a dinner party lately?" he said after a moment.

She looked at him, confused. "What?"

"A dinner party. Food. Dancing. Music."

"Oh, yes." It was like him to change the conversation. She knew she had said as much as she could in one day.

"I shall leave the details to you, of course."

"Of course."

"Ah, there is Lord Wriothesley and Bishop Gardiner," he said, nodding at two men who approached them from another path. "Do be sure we have quail this time."

He kissed her cheek lightly. "Farewell, my dear Kate."

She curtseyed before the visitors, then lifted her skirts and strolled calmly back down the long, shrub-lined corridor. But as soon as she was out of sight, she leaned against the hedge, her heart beating rapidly. "Foolish. Foolish!" she chided herself. "I must be more careful. He was not so happy with our conversation this time."

At the fountain, Lord Wriothesley and Bishop Gardiner greeted the king. He was still seated on the bench, rubbing his knee.

"God be with you, my king," said Bishop Gardiner. His bowed head made his double chin more pronounced.

"A bad day for the gout, Sire?" asked Lord Wriothesley. His heavy mustache quivered as he spoke.

"I am fine," Henry insisted. But his eyes said differently.

"Might I inquire as to the queen's health?" said Gardiner. "She appeared to be distraught."

Henry threw up his hands. "A bad sign it is when women become clergy and I find myself in my old age being taught by my wife!"

"Ah." Gardiner and Wriothesley exchanged glances.

"Your Majesty," said the bishop, "as the Lord Chancellor and I were already in the garden, we could not help overhearing your conversation with the queen."

Since Henry didn't reply, he continued. "I would not offer my counsel if you did not regularly seek it."

"What is it you wish to say to me, Bishop?"

Gardiner cleared his throat. "Your Majesty excels above the princes and doctors of divinity. It is impolite for any subject to argue with you about religion as the queen has. It was pure disobedience."

Henry winced as another pain shot up his leg. Gardiner paused and looked at Lord Wriothesley for help.

"Sire, we know this is unpleasant news," said Wriothesley, "but we have reason to believe that the queen is connected to the Reformed, especially Anne Askew." He paused, stroking his mustache as he waited for his words to sink in. "Their religion destroys governments and their leaders, ignoring your God-given rights to rule. Surely, in your great wisdom, you can see that it is perilous to cherish a serpent so near to your breast."

"What is your point?" demanded Henry, his face reddening.

Gardiner cleared his throat again. "What the Lord Chancellor is trying to say is that the queen has, in defending the rights of the Reformed and considering their teachings, violated your laws. Though it is shocking to say so, it is our duty to inform you that she has"—he paused dramatically— "committed treason."

Henry grunted. "That is nonsense, Stephen. It is an insult to the queen and therefore an insult to me."

"I mean no ill will, Your Majesty," the bishop replied with a small bow. "My heart is dedicated to the Church of England and committed to your just rule. But if the Reformed are allowed to continue, that rule may be in jeopardy."

"What proof do you have to support your charges?"

"Evidence is being collected as we speak," said Wriothesley.

"Show me your proof," the king barked at them. He struggled to his feet. "*If* the queen is guilty of heresy, I will sign articles of her arrest. Good day, gentlemen."

They bowed ceremoniously and watched as he limped back to the garden entrance, where two of his guards were waiting for him.

The next day, Katherine met Henry in the garden as usual. She immediately told him she had made the arrangements for his dinner party. That put him in a good mood, though he was still favoring his leg.

But soon she opened a new subject. "I have heard it suggested that the Church of England ought to establish an official English translation of the Bible."

He was paying attention now, and scanned the garden uneasily. "Where would you hear such a thing?"

"I hear the rumblings of the court."

"And what is your opinion?"

"I dare not presume to know what is best for the English people, as that is your right."

"But?"

She smiled. "But for myself, I might see the spiritual benefit in being able to read the Holy Scriptures in my own language. I am not as proficient in Latin as the king."

He spoke without looking at her. "You choose your words with care, my dear Kate, but what you advocate is a Reformed idea."

"I wonder if it matters whose idea it is?" She turned her small earnest face toward him. "Ought not the Church of England consider any ideas which glorify Christ, no matter the source?"

He towered over her and fixed her with a stern gaze. "*I* am the Church of England!" he roared. "I will not allow her to fall prey to heresy. I suggest that you avoid court gossip altogether if it causes you to repeat the ideas of heretics."

"Yes, my lord." She had reached the limit of conversation much more quickly today.

He limped forward again, and she tried to concentrate as he began to discuss the state of his forests.

She let the subject go for a few days, hoping to bring it up again when the king's leg was better. But by the end of the week, Agnes and a few of Katherine's other ladies-in-waiting were arrested.

When they heard the news, Margaret and Rose, another woman of the court, fled to Katherine's suite. But the queen had not sent for them. They waited outside the entrance, whispering.

"The bishop searched Agnes' house for banned books."

"Did he find anything?"

"I don't know. I can only hope she was sensible enough not to leave any Reformed pamphlets lying about."

"Shh! Someone's coming."

Boots rang in the corridor. The women folded their hands and looked at the queen's door as though they expected it to open.

Henry's messenger passed them. Margaret looked him right in the eye, hoping his expression would tell her something about what was going on, but he just nodded and wished them a good morning.

He was nearly out of sight when she noticed the crumpled bit of paper at her feet.

"Sir, you dropped something," she called after him. But he walked faster and rounded a corner as though he hadn't heard her. She picked it up.

"What is it?" said Rose.

"It looks like an official document," said Margaret, noting the paper. "But I dare not read it. He is the king's messenger."

"The king's messenger does not drop messages accidentally. He must have meant you to see it."

They looked at each other.

"Open it!" urged Rose.

Margaret glanced down the corridor, then smoothed out the crumpled paper. Her mouth dropped open.

"What? What is it?" cried Rose, snatching it away.

"They're going to arrest the queen," she replied, sinking against the wall. "We have to show her this immediately."

This time, they didn't wait to be summoned, but rushed into the queen's suite and past her astonished servant. They found her in her bedchamber at her writing desk.

She looked up in surprise. "What is it? Do you have news about Agnes?"

Margaret shook her head. Rose dropped the paper on the desk.

Katherine stared at it without touching it. It took her a moment to realize it was an order for her arrest, signed by her husband. "Henry!" she exclaimed.

"It was just a matter of time. Henry discards all of his wives!" cried Rose.

Margaret slapped her. "Shh! Don't say such things!"

Katherine had gone as pale as her nightgown. She picked up the arrest warrant with a trembling hand and was suddenly aware of the stack of papers below it she had been working on. "Here!" she said, shoving the stack into Margaret's hands. "You must find a place to hide this. But not in your house—they are bound to search there, if they have not already."

"What is it?" asked Margaret.

Across the top page, in Katherine's delicate handwriting, was written *The Lamentation or Complaint of a Sinner*.

"It is a book—my book," said Katherine quietly, through white lips. "In it I tell of how I was converted to the Reformed faith, and I call the entire English nation to do so as well."

Margaret stared at her as though she was out of her mind. "This is your death certificate!" she cried. "If Bishop Gardiner finds it, there will be no saving you."

"Then he must not find it now. But do not destroy it, for someday I will publish it." She closed her eyes and pressed her fingers to her temples.

"My queen, you look ill," said Rose, kneeling beside the desk chair.

"Call Dr. Wendy," Katherine whispered.

"I'll wait for him," Margaret said to Rose, pressing the stack of paper into her hands. "Go hide that book! And burn this arrest warrant—no one must know we have seen it!"

Rose fled with her arms wrapped around the manuscript. Margaret helped Katherine into bed while the chambermaid ran to call for the doctor.

"Henry," Katherine mumbled. "I did not believe you would go so far!"

Margaret loosened the queen's gown and drew the bed curtains.

Attendants gathered outside the door, but when Dr. Wendy arrived, he sent them all away except Margaret.

"She won't stop shaking," Margaret said, as the doctor came to the bedside. "And her breathing is shallow."

"What brought this on, Katherine?" he asked, leaning in to listen to her breathe.

The queen did not reply.

He drew Margaret aside. "What happened?"

"The queen received shocking news."

"Then you heard about Anne?"

"Anne?" murmured the queen, struggling to raise herself from her pillows. "What about Anne?"

"I'm sorry, my queen. Anne has been sentenced to death."

Katherine fell back with a moan.

Margaret's hand flew to her mouth. "The queen cannot take this news, Doctor. Not now."

"What happened, Margaret?"

"Katherine just learned that the king has ordered her arrest."

The doctor squeezed his eyes shut. "I had hoped I could convince his majesty to reverse that order before it was carried out."

"You knew?" said Margaret.

The doctor turned back to his patient. "You and the king are keeping me busy today, Katherine. He has a stomach flu, but I know that as soon as he learns of your illness, he will come. I will deliver the message myself."

He turned to Margaret. "There is no point in going anywhere. The arrest is scheduled for two days from now. Make her rest. I am concerned for her heart. You know it has never been strong."

"Will she recover?" asked Margaret.

"If she rests she'll be fine." Dr. Wendy tugged at his beard. "I have an idea."

Katherine's voice was barely audible from the pillows. "Your last idea has earned me a cell in the Tower of London."

"My queen, I believe the king might be influenced to call off your arrest."

The queen's half-closed eyes met the doctor's.

"What do you mean?" insisted Margaret.

"This morning, the king told me you were to be arrested. He swore me to secrecy. How did *you* find out?"

The queen's lady hesitated, but then explained about the dropped message.

"You see?" said the doctor, breaking into a hopeful smile. "Henry made sure I, the queen's doctor, knew about the warrant. Then his messenger *accidentally* dropped a copy outside the queen's door."

"The king wanted us to find out!" said Margaret, dropping to Katherine's bed and taking her hand.

"But why then did he sign for my arrest?" asked Katherine.

"Perhaps to send you a message," said Dr. Wendy. "He told me that he couldn't bear living with a doctress any longer, always telling him what to believe. Perhaps he wanted to frighten you away from your Reformed ideas."

"He has nearly succeeded," replied Katherine.

"No," urged Dr. Wendy. "You have advanced the Reformed cause in a way no one else can do."

Katherine shook her head weakly.

"Hear me out," he insisted. "The king has a soft spot for you, like I never saw with his other wives. He respects you. If he didn't, he never would have tolerated your prodding every day. He's just under the influence of Gardiner and Wriothesley. You need to get back in his good graces."

"How?" Margaret demanded.

"Perhaps he only wants you to apologize."

Katherine frowned. "For believing the truth?"

"For telling the king what to do."

"I've made no demands, only suggestions. I thought he enjoyed our conversations."

"You know better than anyone how fragile his ego is. Kings don't want to be challenged by anyone, especially their wives."

Margaret stroked the queen's hand. "The doctor is right. Perhaps if you beg the king's forgiveness, he'll repeal the warrant."

"And then what?"

"And then you will live to promote the Reformed cause some other way. Stay in bed and rest," Dr. Wendy commanded, picking up his hat. "I will get the king to come to you."

A few hours later, Henry arrived at the queen's suite. Margaret had cleaned off her writing table and the polished surface was empty now. The bed hangings were pulled back. When the king saw his wife sobbing in her bed, he limped to her side as quickly as possible. "My sweet Kate, what has happened?"

"I have fallen ill, my husband," she said, not looking at him.

He responded by gently brushing a lock of damp hair behind her ear.

"I fear I have displeased you and now you have forsaken me."

"Blot the tears from your eyes, my dear," he said, handing her his handkerchief. "You are not forsaken."

He sat with her for an hour, while Dr. Wendy stood outside the door. Before Henry left, he stopped to have a word with the doctor.

"What did he say?" Katherine wanted to know when the doctor returned to her room.

"He demanded that I take good care of you." He smiled. "I was right about him. He is not eager for your arrest. He just wants to prove to his advisors that you are willing to submit to him, that he rules everyone, including his wife."

She took a deep breath and sat up. "I am sorry that he chooses to carry his burdens alone. But I am willing to humble myself for the sake of the gospel."

"Yes?"

"I will visit the king publicly and declare my obedience. For my sake and that of my imprisoned ladies, you must pray for my success."

"Of course, my queen."

"Thank you, good doctor."

He bowed, and left the room. Margaret appeared in the doorway.

"Margaret," Katherine called, waving her to the bed. "Be sure that Rose has carefully hidden my book. Tell my ladies that, for now, all ideas and books of the Reformed are out of the question."

"My queen?"

"Now is not the time to pressure the king. Go—and pray," she insisted. "I must rest now, for tomorrow I visit the king."

She fell back on the pillows and began to pray.

Henry was holding court with his counselors the next day when the court crier announced the presence of the queen. The counselors frowned at the interruption, but the king looked pleased.

The men parted as she made her way down the long aisle to the throne. She was dressed in full royal costume with a stiff lace collar, jeweled necklace, and hair smoothed back under a beaded veil.

"The queen graces us with her presence," Henry declared.

She smiled at him and curtseyed.

"You must have something on your mind," he prompted. "What business do you bring to the court?"

"Your Majesty knows that I am ignorant and imperfect," said Katherine, her fair eyelashes lowered. "It is my status in life to be subject to you, my king, but I fear I have not demonstrated that properly."

The men in the room were stunned at her confession. They turned to see how the king would respond.

"Indeed, you have become a doctor, my dear," he said, straightening his shoulders. "You have attempted to instruct me in the ways of the church rather than be instructed by me."

The counselors nodded their agreement. They had heard such unpleasant rumors.

"If Your Majesty has understood my intentions in this way," replied Katherine, "then Your Majesty has misunderstood me. I have not meant to teach my husband. Rather, my love has emboldened me to speak with you because I thought our lively conversations took your mind off of your pain. I have learned much from our discussions. I assure Your Majesty that I defer to your wisdom, as all Your Majesty's subjects ought."

The counselors straightened their tunics and looked knowingly at one another. It was time this queen acknowledged her place!

The king did not miss their reaction. Stiffly, he pulled himself to his feet. "Then perfect friends we are now again, my dear, as ever we were before." He reached out and took the hand she offered, kissing it regally. "Hearing your words is better than a hundred thousand pounds falling into my pocket! I will never question your loyalty to me again."

The words were for show, she knew, but she saw true pleasure in his eyes.

"Your Majesty is infinitely gracious," she said, curtseying again. Turning to face the court, she straightened the train of her gown and proceeded with dignity back down the aisle.

Margaret followed her to her suite, where they wept with relief together.

The following morning, Katherine again found the king waiting for her at the entrance to the garden. The skies threatened rain, but the paths were still dry. Forget-me-nots nodded in the breeze.

It was the day scheduled for her arrest. She knew that her visit to the king yesterday had won his favor, but even the king could not cancel his orders.

Henry offered her his arm. She took it gratefully, and matched her pace to his limp. As they strolled between the hedges, she said little but listened as he described a letter from Prince Edward.

Margaret and Rose insisted on following them at a discreet distance, as did several of the king's men. They kept glancing behind them, expecting to see soldiers, but the paths were clear. Margaret began to relax. But when they turned at the far side of the garden, Chancellor Wriothesley was approaching from behind them with forty soldiers.

Katherine drew in a sharp breath and tightened her grip on the king's arm. He clasped a warm hand over hers and squeezed it. They stood still, waiting in silence.

"I beg Your Majesty's pardon," said Wriothesley, holding out a sheet of paper as he closed in on them. "This is a warrant for the queen's arrest."

Katherine's ladies and Henry's men stepped in closer to the king and queen. The soldiers hesitated behind the chancellor.

"Sire?" prompted Wriothesley.

The king released his wife's arm and drew himself to his full height. "Fool!" he declared, advancing slowly on the chancellor, dragging his leg behind him. "How dare you interrupt my walk?"

Wriothesley dropped to his knees with a bewildered look. "But, Your Majesty, we have a legal warrant for the arrest of the queen. It is signed by your own hand!"

"You call my wife a traitor?" The king snatched the document away and tore it in half. "Get out of my garden!" he snarled, his face purple. "If you value your life, never visit me again."

The chancellor's whiskered jaw fell open in astonishment. With the king staring him down, he turned and fled the garden. His confused soldiers followed.

The king took a deep breath, adjusted his belt, and straightened his shoulders. Turning back to Katherine, he offered her his arm again and continued down the path.

He saw in her eyes that she knew what had taken place, but she did not question him.

"Don't worry, my dear," he said. "Wriothesely will not trouble you again."

"I'm sure the good chancellor must have acted out of ignorance rather than evil will."

Henry gave a short laugh. "Ah, Kate, how little you know about politics."

Katherine glanced at Margaret behind her, a slight smile touching her lips. "Yes, Your Majesty, how little I know. Now, what shall we talk about today?"

On July 16, 1546, Anne Askew was burned at the stake, refusing to name the queen and other members of the court who were secretly Reformed.

The following January, Henry VIII died, leaving England to his son, Edward VI. Katherine had convinced Henry to name as his son's guardian a reform-minded man, Edward Somerset, who with Archbishop Thomas Cranmer influenced the young King Edward to further separate the Church of England from Rome.

Shortly after Henry's death, Katherine published her book The Lamentation or Complaint of a Sinner *and married her former fiancé, Sir Thomas Seymour. She died giving birth in September of 1548.*

Thomas Cranmer: Candles in England

OCTOBER 16, 1555. OXFORD, ENGLAND.

JUST OUTSIDE OF Balliol College, a sober crowd watched as two men were led by soldiers to an iron stake in the courtyard surrounded by a bed of sticks. Both men wore the long black gowns and velvet caps of university professors.

"This is it, Ridley. May the end come quickly," said the older man.

"Be cheerful, Latimer," said his younger friend. "God will either halt the flames or give us the strength to endure them."

On a platform in the midst of the crowd sat a row of officials. At each corner of the platform, an armed soldier kept a watchful eye on the crowd, prepared for rioting. Already demonstrators were shouting "Release them!" even as others shouted "Burn the Reformed heretics!"

"Lord Williams!" Ridley cried from the pile of sticks. "Lord Williams, I ask you for Christ's sake that I may speak a word or two."

The magistrate rose from his chair on the platform. "If you, Master Nicholas Ridley and Master Hugh Latimer," his voice rang out over the people, "will recant your false beliefs, you will be allowed to speak. You may yet save your life."

"I will not turn my back on Christ's truth," shouted Ridley defiantly. "God will judge Master Latimer and I fairly."

Lord Williams shrugged. "Very well then. We are done here." He nodded to the soldiers, who locked Latimer and Ridley in irons at the stake.

A man approached the two accused men and hung small pouches around their necks. The crowd hastily backed away.

"What are these?" demanded Ridley.

"Gunpowder bags," the man replied. "They will ensure that you die as quickly and painlessly as possible."

"If it will help me get to Christ sooner, I welcome it," declared Latimer. He looked Ridley in the eye. "Be of good comfort, Master Ridley, and play the man; we shall this day light such a candle by God's grace in England, as I trust shall never be put out."

Lord Williams waved a hand, and the candles were lit.

From an upper window of Bocardo Prison, in the north gate of Oxford, an old man watched the fireworks with tears streaming down his cheeks.

"Ridley! Latimer!" he cried, tearing the cap off his head and falling to his knees. He choked on the smell of the burning gunpowder. Tears streamed down his thin cheeks and soaked his long white beard.

"Come now, Master Cranmer." The two prison guards lifted the old man by the elbow. "The crowd down there is getting out of hand. You must return to your cell now."

They led him to the door, but his weeping eyes remained fixed on the window where he had witnessed his friends' fate.

For many days, he prayed feverishly from the hard floor of his dark cell. Cold despair fell over him like a mountain's shadow. "I'm next!" he thought. "The next time it will be me tied to the stake. What am I to do?"

He stared at his hands that still bore the rings of the highest-ranking church official in England. The sight threw him into another fit of weeping. "Who am I to think I don't deserve this? I condemned others when I was archbishop!"

His days as Archbishop of Canterbury seemed like dreams of someone else's life. He had been the religious advisor and faithful servant of Henry VIII, King of England. Henry had no intention of being subject to the pope, and insisted it was his right as king—not the pope—to be head of the church in England. He was not willing to break completely with Rome, but his attitude gave Archbishop Cranmer the opportunity to steer the king and his country toward Reformed thinking. Under Henry's authority, Cranmer preached about the errors of the pope and wrote a new book of prayers for the English people.

But he had not had the courage to stand up to Henry when the king repeatedly divorced or executed his wives and remarried. The face of Anne Boleyn and the other discarded queens still tortured his memory.

After Henry died, Prince Edward carried on with his father's ideas, encouraged by his stepmother, Queen Katharine Parr. Archbishop Cranmer served Edward as he had served Henry. With his help, Edward further separated the Church of England from the Church of Rome. But Edward's reign was short and he died young.

"And that is when my fortunes changed!" remembered the former archbishop bitterly.

He had followed Edward's orders to crown Lady Jane Grey, a royal cousin and a Reformed sympathizer, as queen after Edward died. But Edward's sister Mary was next in line to the throne. Furious, she gathered an army. Six days after Jane had become queen, Mary took London by force. She crowned herself queen, declared England a Roman Catholic nation, and imprisoned all the Reformed supporters she could find.

Cranmer and Jane were tried and condemned for treason. Jane was beheaded. But Mary sent Cranmer to Oxford and imprisoned him with Reformed professors Ridley and Latimer.

"And now even my beloved cellmates are gone!" he thought.

The man who was once England's spiritual leader was now a condemned heretic. Instead of preaching from his beautiful pulpit at Canterbury Cathedral, he stared at the brick walls of his cell. Instead of browsing the bookshelves in his personal library, he fingered the worn pages of the one prayer book he was allowed. Instead of advising young scholars and going home to his wife and children, he sat alone day and night in the confines of his prison.

He could not have been more miserable.

One morning, his cell door clanked, then pushed open unexpectedly. "Your sister is here to see you," the soldier announced.

A woman rushed to embrace him. She wore the habit of a nun. "It is good to see you, Thomas!" she said.

He willed his aging knees to rise. "Dear Alice!" He held on to her desperately, grateful for the touch of another human being.

"I have good news," she said. "I've managed to convince the queen that your rights are being violated. This cell is inappropriate for someone of your stature."

He shook his head sadly. "Mary will never let me return to my home."

"Well, no, under the circumstances," admitted Alice. "But when I reminded Her Excellency of your faithful devotion to her father, she was inclined to move you to a friendlier environment."

"Where?" he demanded.

"You will stay with the dean at Christ Church."

His eyes widened in surprise. "Christ Church! That is hardly a prison."

She smiled. "You will remain under guard at all times. But the company of scholars should cheer you up, yes?"

He took her hand in his. "Thank you, dear sister. You cannot know how wretched the last few months have been! But, I still don't understand."

"You believed the queen incapable of mercy?"

"She condemned me to die as a traitor!"

His sister looked away. "You made your choices, Thomas."

"My choice was to obey my sovereign. I did everything in my power to keep Edward's will, including resisting Mary's usurpation of the throne."

"My brother, why won't you just walk away from this silliness? All you need to do is turn away from the Reformed doctrine and Mary will forgive you."

"I cannot," said Thomas, shaking his head firmly. "The supper of the Lord as taught by Rome is unbiblical. The pope is not above Scripture, even if the queen says so."

"You are challenging centuries of established teaching in the church."

"If that teaching contradicts the Holy Scripture, then it is right to challenge the church!"

"You were once a respected leader of that church, dear brother. Don't you see how your rebellious actions have ruined your life?"

"I have done many things I regret, Alice. I must follow my conscience now."

"What about your family?"

"They are being cared for. I miss them, but I have trusted them to the Lord."

A knock came at the door.

"I must go now," she said. "But please, reconsider."

As soon as she left, he returned to his knees, this time to thank God that he would soon be delivered from his cell.

The dean of the college was waiting for him in the great hall when he arrived. "Welcome to Christ Church," said the dean. "I'm Richard Marshall. I trust you'll find your stay here far more pleasant than Bocardo Prison."

"Yes, I already do." His eyes took in the beautiful paneled walls and high stone windows that let in wide beams of light.

"I am under strict orders from Her Majesty. You will be allowed daily walks outside, but your access will be limited. We have prepared comfortable quarters."

"Thank you."

"I have business to attend to, so I will waste no time in introducing you to Nicholas Woodson." He gestured to the young man beside him. "He will be responsible for your guard. Let him know if you need anything. If it is permitted, he will oblige."

"Thank you," Thomas said again.

The dean hurried away.

Nicholas stretched out his arm. "This way, Master Cranmer."

They left the great hall and crossed an open courtyard to a series of chambers. Nicholas respectfully matched his pace to the old man. As they passed a cluster of clergymen discussing a passage of the gospel of John, the conversation broke off and the men stared at them. One of the older men nodded politely. Thomas knew they must have recognized their former archbishop.

"Fresh air, scholarly conversations, respect for my office," he thought. "It is almost as it used to be." He sighed deeply.

The room Nicholas led him to was larger than his cell at Bocardo. A rug covered the floor, and a wool blanket had been smoothed across the low bed. Thomas was most delighted to see a small stack of books on the narrow desk.

"I have stocked your desk with paper and ink," said Nicholas. "However, your letters will be reviewed before they are posted. Her Majesty has ordered us to limit your contact with the outside."

"I understand. Thank you for your kindness."

Nicholas nodded. "I will have food sent to you shortly, and then you may wish to rest. I will return tomorrow to see what else you need." He left.

Rejoicing at the change in his circumstances, Thomas picked up one of the little volumes and sat down to read until his meal arrived.

Over the next few days, Thomas saw a lot of Nicholas. The young man made sure his food was hot and his clothing was clean. He brought him more books when he had read all the others. When the weather was clear, they went for walks in the courtyard and often stopped to talk to the other scholars.

The image of his friends dying at the stake began to fade from his dreams. He had forgotten what it was like to sleep through the night.

"You are looking healthier now than when you arrived," said Nicholas one evening. They had taken supper together and were sitting in Thomas's room.

"The result of these delightful puddings you've been bringing me," Thomas replied, glancing at his empty plate. "We did not have much of a cook at Bocardo."

Nicholas laughed. "Put those days behind you forever, Master Cranmer." He leaned forward. "Return to the church. You've spent time with me and the others these last few days. Surely you can see we aren't the demons you Reformed have painted us as over the years."

"You are a good man, Nicholas," assured Thomas, "but even good men can be wrong."

"Then might you not be wrong as well?"

"Can you show me from the Word of God where I am wrong?"

"I will not presume to teach a master such as yourself. But you will have an opportunity to re-think your doctrine tomorrow."

"Tomorrow?" Thomas looked at him sharply. "What happens tomorrow?"

"You have been called to an audience with Pedro de Soto and

Juan de Villagarcia, Dominican friars who are professors here at the university."

"I am to stand trial again?" Agitated, he knocked over his mug.

Nicholas stooped to retrieve it. "No, Master Cranmer, not a trial. Just another chance to discuss your beliefs and be restored to the church."

Thomas groaned. "Young man, that is a trial." He shook his head. "I should have known all this was too good to be true."

"Just listen to what they have to say."

"I'm a prisoner here. I have no choice but to listen!"

Nicholas stood. "The meeting will be at the dean's house. I'll come to get you when it's time."

Worried, Thomas prayed longer than usual that night and went to bed with a heavy heart.

Nicholas accompanied him to the dean's house the next day, where the two professors were waiting for him. They wore the black cloaks that identified the Dominican order and sat in ornate chairs perched on a platform. A third chair had been placed below them in the center of the room. It was to be a private meeting.

"Please have a seat," said Friar de Soto. He had a strong Spanish accent.

Thomas sat.

Friar Villagarcia wasted no time. He drew his heavy eyebrows together and leaned forward in his seat. "You reject the Lord's supper, no?"

Thomas took a deep breath. "I do not reject the Lord's supper," he insisted calmly. "I reject the teachings of the pope on the Lord's supper, where those teachings differ from Scripture."

The friar chose a different question. "You permit your priests to marry though the church forbids it?"

"I permit what the Scripture does not forbid," the former archbishop said gravely. "Unless you are aware of a secret book of the Bible?"

Villagarcia frowned.

De Soto picked up the questioning. "Why do you reject the mass?" he demanded.

"I reject it because I trust in Christ alone for my salvation, not the mass," answered Thomas. "That is what Scripture teaches."

"As God's representative, the pope determines what Scripture says."

"The pope is the antichrist!" declared Thomas. "That is what happens when one man believes he has all power over the church."

De Soto flinched. "If not the pope, then who should be in charge? Or do you prefer disorder in the kingdom of God?"

"The church fathers called councils, like the Council of Nicea. They agree as one in the Spirit of Christ."

"Ah, but who calls church councils?"

Thomas looked at him as though the friar was hard of hearing. "I just said the church does."

"Who specifically?"

"What are you getting at?"

The corners of de Soto's mouth turned up in a cold smile. "You say that the church decides official doctrines based on church councils. You are right, of course. But someone must call that council in the first place. If the pope convenes the council, does that not prove he has the ultimate authority over that council?"

"Well, in recent times the pope has taken it upon himself to call councils. But that is because he is corrupt. The first great council of the church was not called by a pope, but by agreement of the church fathers."

"You are certain of this?"

Thomas's eyes narrowed. "I am as learned a man as you, Friar. If you can prove that a pope called the first great council of the church, I will concede that he is the head of the church indeed."

De Soto stood abruptly. "Very well then. We will re-convene shortly."

The two friars hurried out of the room. When they returned a short time later, they brought a box of papers and Dean Marshall.

Villagarcia began. "Master Cranmer, for the dean's sake, I ask you again. Will you concede that the pope is the head of the church if we can prove that a pope called the first general council of the church?"

"If you could prove it, I would concede," stated Thomas confidently.

"Very well." The friar held up a book. "Here is an ancient text from a church father who said that the first council of Nicea was called by Pope Sylvester I. So, the pope did call the first council after all, and therefore he must have the greater authority."

Thomas grabbed the book furiously. "This writer lived after the council and does not know the history. No reliable church father makes such a claim. This is just propaganda of the Roman church, not proof!"

"You see?" shouted Villagarcia. "He hears the truth and he finds a conspiracy in it. No wonder the queen has declared him a heretic." He gestured to Nicholas. "Take him away."

Nicholas was quiet until they reached the door to Thomas's room. "Wasn't there a day when all the church teachings seemed right to you, Master Cranmer?" he asked as he opened the door.

The old man went inside. "Yes, there was. But the Holy Spirit showed me I was wrong."

Nicholas followed him in. "What if you are wrong now? Perhaps you've just spent too much time around the Reformed."

"I don't think so."

Nicholas looked at him earnestly. "But you believe in the divine right of kings and queens to rule, do you not?"

"Yes."

"So if the queen commands you to follow the teachings of the pope, is it not a sin to disobey?"

Thomas shrugged his shoulders. "Is it not a sin to follow a corrupt pope?"

"Is not the unity of the church of Christ more important than the corruption of one pope?"

"No! Yes. Maybe." He sighed and sank down on his bed. "I don't know anymore." He looked around his comfortable room and at the genuine concern on the young man's face. "Nicholas, you've been kind to me. Maybe you are right. When I'm here, talking to you and the other scholars, everything seems right."

Nicholas was hopeful. "Would you be willing to attend mass with me?"

"I've rejected the mass," reminded Thomas.

"But the mass is only an extension of the work of Christ. You are not rejecting him by attending."

The old man hesitated. "Well——."

"It will allow you to reassess your thoughts on it," Nicholas interrupted. "You haven't been to one in a long while."

Thomas sighed again. "Alright, Nicholas. For the sake of confirming my views, and for your friendship, I will go with you." But the decision made him uneasy.

He was even more unhappy when he got back to his room after the mass. The service was familiar, but he felt like a betrayer. "Heavenly Father," he prayed that night, "what am I to do? My heart is in confusion."

He was soon called to the dean's house for another meeting with the friars.

"I hear you went to mass," began Villagarcia. "Have you reconsidered our argument?"

Nicholas urged his friend in a loud whisper. "Come on, Thomas, surely you've given some thought to our conversation."

"Master Cranmer, do you choose the fires of hell or love of the church?" Villagarcia's voice grew irritated.

"The pope is not the head of the church," said Thomas.

"Master, think carefully," said Nicholas. He turned to Villagarcia. "These are serious issues, Master Villagarcia. Master Cranmer is wrestling with himself to come to the truth. Please give him more time."

"More time!" shouted Villagarcia. "We've shown you polite company and good meals, Cranmer. We've given you plenty of time to consider your position on these issues. Do you really need more time?"

Thomas's eyes narrowed and he leaned in closer. "No amount of time will convince me of your errors!"

While Villagarcia sputtered, de Soto jumped in. "Clearly Master Cranmer has not recanted from his Reformed heresy. I see no point in continuing. Nicholas, return him to his room."

Nicholas led him outside, but Thomas had a hard time keeping up with him. As soon as they reached the door to Thomas's room, the young man flung it open and turned on him furiously. "I have shown you every kindness here. I have tried to convince you of your errors and make the consequences easier on you. And this is how you repay my friendship?"

He slammed the door shut on Thomas and turned the key firmly in the lock.

For three days, Thomas heard and saw nothing of Nicholas. An unknown young man brought him food, but he was not allowed to leave his room and he had no company. At night, he tossed in his bed, hearing Villagarcia's voice crying, "fires of hell!" Images of his friends at the stake filled his dreams again.

He got out of bed and eased his aching knees onto the hard floor. "My gracious Father in heaven," he prayed. "Your name is holy and my lips are sinful. What am I to do? Am I being foolish? Am I rejecting your church? Send me your wisdom and grace, my Lord. For I need them more than ever before. Amen."

Morning was beginning to dawn outside his window when Thomas rose from his prayers and sat down at his small desk. He had just enough light to find a sheet of writing paper and an inkwell. "My good friend Nicholas," he wrote. "Forgive my actions the other day. I do appreciate your friendship and patience with me. Please come back and spend the day with me. I desire to talk with you again, my friend."

A guard answered his knock immediately and promised to deliver the letter right away. An hour later, Nicholas appeared at his door with breakfast.

"I am so glad you have come!" cried Thomas. "I have been quite lonely without your conversation."

"As have I," the young man admitted, setting the tray on the desk.

Thomas dragged the chair closer to the bed and sat on the edge. "Please sit and enjoy this food with me. What shall we talk about today?"

Nicholas remained standing. "I want to maintain our friendship, Master Cranmer, but you understand that I cannot regard a heretic as my brother."

Thomas looked down and fidgeted with the tray. "Perhaps another subject would be better, my friend. Have you written any sermons lately? Received any interesting letters?"

"This is no time for small talk. Your very survival is in the hands of Villagarcia and De Soto! You must pull yourself together and rejoin us."

Thomas set down his cup with a trembling hand. His reply was quiet. "I don't want to be out of fellowship with you or the church, Nicholas. I do believe in unity! But the queen asks me to give up all I have worked for my whole life. That is no small matter."

"It is no small matter that you will be executed for heresy!"

"I have asked the Lord to show mercy on me and change the queen's heart. In the meantime, can we not sit and talk like old times?"

Nicholas threw up his hands. "If you do not care to save your life, why should I try? There is no more to be said between us. Good bye." He crossed the room in three steps and flung open the door.

Thomas stumbled to his feet. "No, don't leave, Nicholas! Come back! You are the only friend I have left! The others—gone—the flames—."

Hearing a crash, Nicholas turned back. Thomas was crumpled on the floor, where he had fainted. The tray and dishes were scattered around him.

He flew to the old man's side. "Master Cranmer!"

The white eyelashes fluttered, and then the watery eyes began to focus. Thomas's lips moved.

"What? I can't hear you, Master."

"My nerves cannot take this strain," Thomas whispered.

"Let me help you up. I will bring you something to drink." He helped the old archbishop into a sitting position.

Thomas waved him away. "No, Nicholas, listen to me. I am too old and too tired to reform the church. I will sign a statement."

"A statement? You mean you will recant?"

"I will give the queen what she wants. Just help me to my desk."

He felt better once he drank the cool water Nicholas brought. When the young man was gone, he sat at the little desk with a quill in his hand and a sheet of paper before him. But he struggled for words. He did not want to compromise what he believed, but he did want to please the queen and her friars.

"I am content to submit myself to your laws," he wrote, "and to the pope as the head of the church—." He paused. He was about to add, "in all things." But was he really willing to submit to the pope in all things? He decided instead to write, "as far as the laws of God and the customs of this kingdom permit."

He added a few other polite lines and then sent the letter off to the queen immediately, before he could change his mind.

But as he thought more about his words, he realized the queen would never accept his statement. It wasn't clear enough. She would still consider him a heretic. So he picked up his pen and wrote a second statement. "I, Thomas Cranmer, doctor of divinity, submit myself to the catholic church of Christ, to the pope, the supreme head of the church, and to the king and queen's majesties, and all their laws."

"Perhaps that will satisfy her," he thought, sending it off by messenger. He stretched out his aching body on the bed and tried to ignore his aching conscience.

But Nicholas brought word that the queen was unimpressed by Thomas's statements. "They're too vague," he explained. "You must clearly denounce the Reformed heresy, not just pledge obedience to the pope."

"How far must I go? Does the queen expect me to condemn Martin Luther and other Reformed teachers?"

"Yes, she does indeed!"

"No." Thomas shook his head. "I can condemn myself, but I will not speak so of God's servants."

"The queen is losing her patience, Master."

"I have already done more than I should! The queen can send me back to Bocardo Prison if she doesn't like it!"

And she did.

In the blackness of his first night back in the miserable little cell, he remembered Nicholas's goodbye. "My friend, love the church and turn from your sins," the young man had said tearfully. He tried to sleep, but the nightmare of his friends burning at the stake returned. His joints throbbed in the damp. For the second time, he had lost his books, fresh air, the joy of companionship.

"No man can take this!" he cried in despair.

In the morning, he called for a sheet of paper and wrote out another statement. "I, Thomas Cranmer, late archbishop of Canterbury, renounce and detest the heresies and errors of Luther and all other teachings contrary to sound doctrine. I confess one holy and catholic church, without which there is no salvation. I acknowledge the pope to be the supreme head of the church on earth, and that all Christians are subject to him. I believe in purgatory and I believe in the Lord's supper as it is taught by the church."

His tears dropped onto the paper as he signed his name to it. "I am a wretched man!" he cried. "A wretched, wretched man."

Friar Villagarcia relished the new statement. But it had come too late. Queen Mary welcomed him back to the church, but he had been convicted of treason, and justice demanded that he be put to death. The former archbishop was sentenced to die at the stake like his friends Ridley and Latimer. He was ordered to make one last recantation of the Reformed faith to read publicly before his execution.

Thomas fell to his knees and wept. "Lord, Heavenly Father," he prayed aloud, "what have I done? I've sold myself to the antichrist and now I'm left to die anyway! Forgive me. Forgive me for I am weak and afraid to die. Show me your eternal mercy. Give me courage now that I may serve you one last time. Amen."

He rose and began to prepare his final statement.

Nicholas came to Bocardo to say goodbye.

"You have been a dear friend to me, Nicholas," said Thomas, embracing his former guard. "You are a good man."

"I wish it did not have to end this way!" said Nicholas.

"The blame is not yours," Thomas insisted calmly. "You have lived by your conscience. I only regret that I have not done so as consistently as you."

"I have arranged for prayers to be said for you at the church, as you requested."

"Thank you. And now, I have one final favor to ask of you." He pulled a sheaf of papers from under his black robe and pressed them into Nicholas's hands like precious treasure. "I have written letters to my wife and children. Also a plea to the queen to restore to me the estates of the archbishopric so that my son may inherit them according to the law."

"I will see that these are delivered straightaway." Nicholas cleared his throat and blinked away the tears. "Master Cranmer——."

"Never fear, Nicholas. God is not done with me yet."

He returned to his prayers as soon as he was alone again.

That night a servant girl delivered his last meal, a small tray of spice cakes and prunes. "Thank you," he told her, pressing a coin into the palm of her hand. "Pray for me tomorrow."

"I am just a servant, Master Cranmer. My prayers can do nothing for you now."

He put a gentle hand on her fair head. "The prayer of a believing servant girl is worth far more than the prayer of a corrupt priest," he told her.

She left him with a promise to pray.

It was raining the next morning. The archbishop knew this was bad news, as rain only prolonged execution by fire. "A final opportunity for courage," Thomas told himself.

He was escorted to the prison gate. Friar Villagarcia and Friar de Soto were waiting for him, their cloaks pulled up around their necks to ward off the drizzle.

"The time has come, Master Cranmer," said Villagarcia. "You have prepared your final statement?"

Thomas did not reply, but handed the friar a sheet of paper like the one rolled into his cloak.

In a low voice, Friar de Soto began to chant a psalm as the three of them made their way toward University Church. The wet streets were lined with people, their faces somber. In the mist, their clothing, their skin, even the buildings on either side of them seemed the same shade of gray.

It was drier and slightly warmer inside the church. Thomas was escorted to the front and kept standing while a sermon was preached warning the people of the evils of Reformed doctrine. The preacher declared that though Master Cranmer had recanted, his execution was the only proper response to his long life of refusing to turn from heresy. The people were told to pray for his soul.

"And now, Master Cranmer will make a final statement," said the preacher. Thomas climbed up to stand beside him.

It had been a long time since he had stood in the pulpit. Looking out over the people crowded into the church, he remembered sermons he had preached, prayers he had led. He had served the Lord's supper to King Henry himself! Now he stood here as a condemned heretic, allowed one final chance to speak to his people.

"Give me courage, Lord," he prayed again silently, and took a deep breath.

"I am a sinner," he began.

The church was silent and his voice boomed across the aisles.

"But I trust in God's mercy." He unrolled the sheet of paper from his belt and spread it across the top of the pulpit.

Villagarcia opened his copy of the statement and began to follow along with his finger.

"And now," Thomas continued, "I come to the great thing that troubles my conscience more than anything I ever did in my life."

Villagarcia nodded. The crowd moved in a little closer to catch every word.

"That great thing that troubles my conscience is not my belief in the Reformed doctrines," cried Thomas. "It is the writing of my recantations! I wrote them out of fear of death, to save my life."

Villagarcia's finger stopped tracing. He turned to De Soto angrily. "This is not what he has written here! This is a false statement. He's not going to recant at all!"

Thomas thundered from the pulpit. "I reject everything I've written in my declining health and mind in prison. For they are untrue!"

"Get him down from there!" shouted Villagarcia. He hurled the statement to the floor and dashed after the guards.

"I do not recant!" shouted Thomas above the din as they dragged him from the pulpit. "I do not follow the pope! He is Christ's enemy!"

The people poured from the church doors into the street as the friars pulled the old man outside.

"Master Cranmer," growled Villagarcia, "you were told to recant. I expected you to try to save your head!"

"That is what I have been doing these many months, and that is what I regret," said Thomas. "But not today! Today I'm finally living by my conscience."

"Clear the way!" shouted Villagarcia. "Clear the way, I said!"

The crowd parted in front of Balliol College, and there, driven into the hard earth, was the iron stake. It was the same spot where Ridley and Latimer had laid down their lives. Thomas looked up and saw the prison window where he had stood and watched them die.

He squeezed his eyes shut. The mist was cold on his face. He could smell the smoky torches prepared to light up the bed of musty straw. But he was no longer afraid of death. He felt freer now than ever before.

He took the stake in his hands and kissed it. Turning to face the crowd, he gazed at the hand with which he had signed his recantations, and thrust it above his head. "The hand which has offended God shall be burned first!"

He hurled his final statement—the real one—into the air. The crowd roared and closed in on him.

"Lord Jesus, receive my spirit," he cried.

Queen Mary printed Thomas Cranmer's recantations as his final words, but Protestant rebels spread his real statement from town to town. Thomas's widow and children were hidden and supported by Reformed friends.

When Mary's Reformed sister Elizabeth became queen in 1558, she declared England a Protestant nation again. She collected Cranmer's scattered papers and letters and had them preserved. The Reformed church in England became a beacon to other nations. Thomas's oldest son eventually reclaimed a portion of his father's estate. Today, many Protestant Christians still use the volume Cranmer wrote during his days as Archbishop of Canterbury, The Book of Common Prayer, as a guide for worship.

JOHN KNOX: TRUMPETER OF GOD

JUNE 4, 1559. ST. ANDREWS, SCOTLAND.

CLUMPS OF TALL sea grass rippled in the wind, pointing up the hill like a road sign. On the rise, two men leading horses stopped to breathe in the salty air.

"Look," said the young well-dressed man. Dropping his horse's lead, he removed his riding gloves and put a hand on the other man's shoulder. "She's exactly where you left her."

His companion, a short man with a sharp nose and a beard so long it covered his chest, peered ahead soberly.

The grasses at their feet stretched out like a green carpet leading to St. Andrews. From this distance, they couldn't tell the university buildings from the blocks of houses. But behind the city, the brown castle towers rose unmistakably from the cliffs into the vast blue sky. They could almost hear the crashing of the North Sea beyond.

"St. Andrews, after all these years," the bearded man said with a sigh. "George Wishart, I've returned."

At the mention of the name, the young man lowered his eyes reverently.

They stood there quietly taking in the view until a shout of "St. Andrews!" broke out behind them.

"Let's continue, Master Knox," said the young man. "The army will catch up with us."

They moved on toward the city as three thousand men came over the rise behind them. The Congregation of Lords was marching on St. Andrews in the name of the Protestant faith.

Knox mopped his brow as he walked. "Lord James, I'm afraid your association with me has not endeared you to the queen regent."

The young lord laughed. "Aye, and my leadership of this militia has?" He shook his dark head. "It saddens me to oppose my own family, but Mary leaves us no choice."

Knox nodded. "She will not allow us to practice our religion in peace!"

"I would have supported her if she would have been willing to compromise. I told her this was a reformation of religion, not politics." But he glanced at the army behind him. "She has made it political. She cannot simply outlaw Protestant preachers like you."

"If something doesn't change, we may all become martyrs for our cause now."

"George Wishart's example is a worthy one to follow!"

"It was in this very city," said Knox, "and at the hands of a cruel cardinal that Wishart's life was taken."

"I don't believe you have ever told me the whole story about you and Wishart. Were you good friends?"

"I was his bodyguard," said Knox. He tapped at his walking stick. "I know you can't tell by looking at me now, but I was once quite good with a two-handed sword!"

"A swordsman! I thought you were a tutor."

"I was. I was responsible for teaching the sons of a number of the Protestant lords that supported Wishart's preaching. Sometimes we traveled together. His sermons caused a stir everywhere—including my soul. That's how I was convinced of the Reformation doctrines. But Wishart was trouble for Cardinal Beaton."

Knox stopped suddenly, color rising in his face. "What kind of cardinal has his own army of mercenaries and a torture chamber?"

"Beaton was proof that the church has become corrupt!" agreed James.

"Aye!" Knox took a deep breath and moved forward again. "We all tried to protect Wishart while he preached across the land. But we failed, and he was captured. The cardinal took him to this very castle and burned him at the stake. I lost my mentor that day."

"But how did you go from being a tutor to a leader of the Protestant movement?"

Knox glanced up the road, judging the distance they had yet to walk. "Let me start at the beginning," he said. "It was thirteen years ago. Our little band was going from town to town, preaching Reformed doctrine in the churches with the cardinal's men hot on our heels. Wishart and I were lodging in Haddington at the time. I had been out that day on business…"

A cold rain had fallen all day, he remembered. A younger Knox picked his way through the streets, avoiding the swelling gutters. He was soaked through, and grateful to see a thin curl of smoke from the chimney as he reached their lodgings. He was anxious to spread his coat before the fire and dry out.

Entering, he found the front room dark. But a group of men were gathered in the back room, whispering—except for Lord Douglas, who apparently didn't know how to whisper. "That would be foolish!" he was shouting as Knox joined them.

"Lower your voice, Douglas," hissed John Cockburn. "Now is not the time for high tempers!"

The men were huddled near the fire. Wishart stood in the middle. His face was strained, and even more pale than usual against his auburn whiskers.

"This can't be good news," said Knox.

"Aye, the worst," replied Wishart.

Cockburn ran a hand through his hair. "Our hope of securing the support of the western lairds is gone."

"We just received an official message from them," explained Douglas. "They're backing out, the cowards!"

Wishart spread his hands. "Many of them have accepted Reformed teaching. But they have families and lands to protect. They're not ready to risk everything for a Protestant government."

"So what do we do now?" asked Knox.

"Continue preaching," Wishart answered immediately. "This is a disappointment, but I can't let it stop me from spreading reformation to my people."

"But the cardinal is after your head! Your safety depends on more than a tutor who doubles as a bodyguard!" Knox touched the sword on his hip.

"My safety can't be your concern anymore, Knox," said Wishart. "This situation requires a change of plans. You are to return to your pupils at Longniddry. Douglas will go with you."

"What? No, I won't," insisted Knox. "Without the western lairds, you're in even more need of our protection!"

Wishart shook his fair head. "Cockburn will remain with me. But the children need you more than I do. I've already taken you away from them for too long."

Knox's voice grew louder. "No, Douglas is right. This *is* foolish!"

Wishart raised a hand to silence him. "Listen, all of you. This is my decision, and I have made it. God has given us each work to do and we must do it." He turned to Cockburn. "See that their horses are prepared. They should leave before it gets too late."

Within the hour, the four men were eating a quick meal together while a servant loaded their horses.

That night, while Knox and Douglas were urging their horses through the rain toward Longniddry, Wishart and Cockburn were captured by Beaton's men and taken to his castle at St. Andrews.

Knox and Douglas heard of the arrest as soon as they reached Longniddry. Douglas went to find friends who might be able to help. But Knox went straight to his pupils.

George and Francis were brothers, sons of Lord Douglas. They were a few years younger than Lord Cockburn's son Alexander, who was nearly eighteen. The three boys had been staying with Protestant supporters while their tutor was away. They were brave, but the news that Alexander's father had been captured made them very glad to see their teacher alive and well.

They sat down immediately when Knox commanded their attention. "Things are looking grim for the followers of the Reformation," he told them.

"Will my father be executed?" Alexander wanted to know. "Can't we rescue him?"

Knox shook his head grimly. "The castle at St. Andrews is built on a steep cliff over the North Sea. The two land-facing sides have high walls surrounded by a ditch. We would need an army to breech the gates, and the lairds are too afraid to rebel. No, we must trust that your father is safe in the hands of God."

"It's not fair!" cried Francis. "More and more of our people are convinced of the Reformed doctrine, and yet the queen and some of our own churchmen persecute us. Why?"

The tutor frowned. It was a question he had asked himself many times. "Some of them believe they are protecting Christ's church from heretics," he said. "If only they could see the truth! Some of them will do anything to stay in power. It is a difficult time for Scotland, boys. We must pray for our bonnie land, and for our friends who have been taken from us."

They were asleep in their beds the next night when they were awakened by shouting outside the house. That was soon followed by urgent pounding on their door.

Knox threw open the gate to find Lord Douglas there with Alexander's father. Lord Cockburn's clothes hung in shreds, and his arms were bleeding.

"Father!" cried Alexander.

"Will you take in a fugitive?" asked Cockburn.

They quickly pulled him inside and slammed the door. Knox sent George to fetch water so Cockburn could clean his wounds.

"How did you escape from Cardinal Beaton?" they demanded.

"It was Wishart he wanted. As soon as we were captured, they dragged him off. There was nothing I could do," Cockburn said, turning to Knox and Douglas. His eyes were red. "They executed him right on the street. Wishart's soldiers said the cardinal watched from a window as George was burned at the stake!"

They all stared at him in horror.

Cockburn looked away. "I was able to get away and ran all night through the woods to get here. I cut up my arms when I fell down a rock ledge."

"But you're alive, thank God!" said Alexander, blotting the blood from his father's arms with a wet towel.

"Yes," said his father. "But now my name is on the cardinal's wanted list. So are yours, gentlemen. Anyone associated with Wishart. Our situation is even more dangerous than before."

Douglas glanced at his sons. "We have to protect the boys."

"We know how to handle swords," said Alexander quickly.

"No, Douglas is right," insisted Cockburn. "Knox, you have to take the boys away from here."

"Father——," began Francis.

"Sit down, son. This is not your decision." Douglas turned to Knox. "We can't stay here with mercenaries looking for us. We're all targets. We need to split up."

Knox leaned forward on his stool. "If the cardinal is looking for me, too, they won't be safer with me."

"They aren't completely safe anywhere," agreed Douglas. "But they're learning about the Reformed faith from you, and that needs to continue." He looked at the three young men with fondness. "They may be our future leaders."

"I'm a tutor," insisted Knox again, "not the leader of a revolution. All I wanted to do after leaving St. Andrews was teach, not fight."

"Three boys do not constitute a revolution, Master Knox," said Douglas.

Knox looked at the boys. He knew Cockburn and Douglas were right about their future. "Aye, we'll go," he said with a sigh. "We'll need money for supplies."

"You'll have it. But prepare quickly. It would be wise for you to leave as soon as possible."

A day later, Knox and the three boys left Longniddry. For seven months, they crossed Scotland, moving from town to town to find safe places to stay while they concentrated on the boys' studies. Every so often, they received messages from the boys' fathers.

One day they received some unexpected news. Cardinal Beaton was dead, rumor had it, and Reformed lords were now in control of his fortified castle at St. Andrews. The governor sent troops to surround it and demand the Reformers surrender, but they refused. So far, people were able to come and go freely.

Could it be that Cardinal Beaton's castle was now the safest place in all of Scotland for Reformed Christians?

Some people thought so. Men that the cardinal had threatened into hiding went back to St. Andrews and joined the castle garrison.

Knox decided to take the boys there with him. He had been educated at the university in St. Andrews, so he knew the region. They had been on the run for too long, and a Reformed haven was just what they needed to focus on their studies.

But when they arrived, the situation wasn't quite what they expected.

The castle was filled with an armed garrison. Filthy soldiers sat around smoky fires drinking beer and shouting jokes at each other. The air was heavy with dust and the stench of sweat, smoke, and stables. The cardinal's once-beautiful chapel was now in ruins, the colored windows smashed and the altar broken into pieces.

Knox demanded to know who was in charge, and went looking for him. The boys stuck close behind him.

The man was taller than most of the soldiers, but just as filthy. "You must be Master John Knox, another of the cardinal's wanted men," the commander said, shaking the teacher's hand with a crushing grip. "I'm John Leslie. Welcome to our piece of Scotland."

"I expected it to be more difficult to gain access to the castle," said Knox.

"We are under a temporary truce," said Leslie. "Has a little something to do with us holding the governor's son hostage."

Knox retracted in surprise. "Hostage?"

"The governor would just as soon kill us as deal with us. But as long as we have his son, we can hold him at bay until English reinforcements arrive to assist us. The boy's in no danger—for now. We've certainly treated him better than the cardinal treated our people!"

"Is Cardinal Beaton really dead?"

"Killed him myself," Leslie said proudly.

"How did you manage to take the castle?"

"George Wishart's murder finally convinced some of the Reformed lords to stand up against Cardinal Beaton," explained Leslie. "So we devised a plan. The cardinal was doing a restoration project on some of the castle walls. One morning, some of our men infiltrated the crew of workmen bringing in limestone. When the drawbridge was lowered, William Kirkcaldy and I distracted the guard, tossed him into the moat, and led our men right into the castle. The cardinal was sleeping in his bed. When we stormed into his room, he actually demanded that we release him because he was a priest. An evil man like that claiming the church to save his neck!"

He paused, and his eyes narrowed in anger. "It was my sword that ended his blasphemy. We threw him in the Bottle Dungeon, like he did to so many innocent people. We were merciful though—he didn't have to go down there alive like his victims!"

Knox paused. He was thinking of Wishart, whose death at the hands of the cardinal had been as violent as the cardinal's own. "It was a just end for Beaton," he agreed. He glanced toward the ruined chapel. "What happened over there? Was there fighting in the chapel?"

Leslie shrugged. "Some of our people refused to stay here with those popish symbols about."

"So they destroyed the house of God?" Knox frowned. "I expected a fellowship of Christians here in St. Andrews, but instead I find gambling, drunkenness, and vandalism."

Leslie shrugged again. "Not everyone is here for the same reason. There are large groups of Reformed Christians looking for shelter from the law here. As long as we can maintain a truce with the governor, we are able to provide that shelter. But this is no monastery, Knox. Accept it as it is, or take your chances outside again."

Knox looked at the boys. "No, we're grateful for your protection. We'll stay out of your way. But I do request access to the cardinal's library."

"Glad to put you in charge of it. The families here will be happy to have a tutor, and I may need someone to compose letters from time to time. Consider it an even trade."

Leslie got someone to find a room for them in one of the towers, and they settled into castle life.

Word spread that a scholar from the university had taken residence in the castle. Knox soon had several more pupils. Every day he worked with them on their studies, focusing especially on Reformed teachings. It was not a perfect environment for learning, but he made the best of it.

One morning, as Knox was testing his students, he got a visit from John Rough. Rough was a thin-faced Reformed preacher who had volunteered to be the garrison chaplain. He and Knox had quickly become friends.

"A word, Master Knox?" Rough asked at the door.

Knox stood. "Boys, Alexander will take over with the questions for a few minutes. You will listen to him and obey."

"Aye, Master Knox," they mumbled.

Knox stepped outside with Rough.

"I need your help," said his friend.

"What is it?"

"I've had sharp dealings with Annand, the local parish priest. I've been teaching the Reformation doctrines to the garrison men, but Annand works to convince them that my teachings are heresy."

"He is a popish priest. What do you expect?"

"I expect that men fighting for the Reformation would ignore this priest and accept Reformed teaching!" exclaimed Rough. "Instead there are many who question my doctrine."

"Not all of us are here for religious reasons. We know some of these men just want to overthrow the government so they can gain power—and the favor of England. It's just politics for them."

"Well, Reformed teachers need to change that."

"What are you asking me to do?"

"Help me preach the doctrines of the Reformation to these men."

Knox shook his head. "I support your work, as I supported Wishart's. But I have no interest in being a minister. I already have a job as a teacher."

"Your reputation as a scholar has spread quickly throughout the entire city. My colleagues and I believe God wants you to use your gifts in the pulpit. People will come to hear you preach."

"Nay," Knox said again. "I'm not a minister."

Rough put a hand on his arm. "This is a call to the church, my friend. One must not refuse the Holy Spirit."

Knox cocked an ear. "I do not hear the Holy Spirit's voice. Only yours." He brushed Rough's hand away and turned back to his classroom. "I already have a responsibility to these children. And I must get back to them now. Good day."

But Rough would not accept his refusal. Every day he told Knox he was called to be a minister. Every day Knox insisted he was a tutor.

A few weeks later, on a Sunday morning, Knox sat with Alexander, George, and Francis in the restored chapel, listening to Rough preach. It just so happened that his sermon was on God's election of ministers.

"The ministry of Christ is a high calling," declared the preacher. "Unless there is a truly biblical reason, no one should refuse a call to church office. Neither for lack of money, time, or desire!"

Knox shifted uncomfortably. "Will he never let this go?" he thought. "How many more Reformed converts he would have if he put his time into teaching them instead of harassing me!"

But Rough was not finished with his sermon. "For the reasons I have declared here today, I call Master John Knox to come forward and accept the call to join me in the ministry of the Word!"

Shouts of approval rose from the congregation.

Knox stared at him. What was Rough thinking? Did he believe he could bully Knox from the pulpit into being a preacher?

Rough glared back. "What do you have to say, Knox? Will you follow in the steps of your brave friend George Wishart?"

Knox jumped up and walked out. Embarrassed, the boys hurried after him.

He went to his favorite place on the wall, a spot where he could look down over the city and see the cathedral and the university. Up on the wall, the salt air refreshed him. Usually there was too much commotion in the castle to hear the surf crash against the eastern cliffs, but on a Sunday morning it was just quiet enough. He let the sound calm him. "Wishart loved St. Andrews," he remembered.

A few paces down the wall, two soldiers on watch glanced in his direction. It was a sober reminder that Scotland was on the brink of civil war in the name of Christ.

Alexander joined him. After a moment he said, "These are troubling times."

"Aye," his teacher replied quietly.

"When I study history with you, I wonder sometimes why God put us in this place at this time."

Knox was silent.

"Master Knox, will you accept the call to ministry?"

"I'm a lawyer, bodyguard, and tutor. Wishart was the preacher."

Alexander looked down over the edge of the wall. "I have learned a great deal from you, Master," he said quietly. "No doubt the Scottish church could learn much from you as well."

He began to walk away, then turned back. "You brought us here to raise leaders among the Reformed. Should it surprise you that they want you as a leader?"

He motioned for the younger boys to follow him, and they left their teacher gazing down at St. Andrews.

For the next few days, no one mentioned the sermon.

Rough continued to have a number of public debates with the priest Annand. Knox thought it was good for the boys to attend these. They could learn more about the Reformed faith while they learned the art of public speaking.

They gathered in the parish church in the city. Rough and Annand rumbled back and forth, arguing about the authority of the pope.

It was hard to sit still and listen to Annand reject their faith, but Knox held his tongue—for a long time. Until Annand declared, "Any teaching outside of the Church of Rome is utterly corrupt!"

Knox was stirred to action. He jumped to his feet and pointed at Annand. "That is a lie," he shouted, "and I can prove it from Scripture!"

Annand raised an eyebrow. "Can you? I know who you are, Master Knox. Are you asking to stand in my pulpit and open the Scriptures to my congregation?"

"Aye, I am," Knox replied firmly.

"Very well," said the priest, calmly shutting the book in his hands and tucking it under one arm. "I'd like to see this proof you claim from Scripture. You shall deliver the sermon this Sunday."

Knox looked at the surprised faces of Rough and Alexander. "Well. Then Sunday it is."

"Sunday it is."

Annand swept out of the pulpit and down the center aisle. Buzzing, the congregation flooded out the center doors. Rough headed down the platform toward Knox, but the tutor was already marching out.

George winked at Francis. They had to run to catch up with their bold teacher.

Knox spent the rest of the week preparing for his sermon. He was used to teaching, but he had never delivered a sermon in front of the faculty of the university. He was nervous.

But Rough assured him that God would not call him to preach and then desert him in the pulpit. "He will give you the words," he insisted. "When the church needs a blast from the trumpet, God equips a trumpeter!"

As soon as he stepped into the pulpit on Sunday, Knox knew Rough was right. The uneasy feeling in his stomach disappeared. All he thought about was the words of Scripture he was called to deliver.

He opened the large Bible on the pulpit to the book of Daniel, chapter seven.

"The prophet Daniel," Knox began, "tells us about the rise of an anti-Christian kingdom in Rome. That kingdom is the Roman church."

Rough nodded vigorously in the front row.

"The popes have become more and more corrupt," Knox continued. "They have abused their power. They have ruled the church as tyrants. They have taught false doctrines not found in the Bible." His voice was rising now. "Scripture declares that we are justified by faith alone, but the pope tells us it is the church that saves us. He thinks he can kick someone out of heaven by excommunicating him from the church. And when someone challenges his authority—like John Wyclif or John Hus—he labels him a heretic and has him burned at the stake. This is not the action of the vicar of Christ!"

The congregation sat on the edge of their seats. They had not heard such impassioned preaching for a long time. Knox read several Scripture passages, explaining how they proved the Reformed faith.

Annand was not happy when Knox stepped out of the pulpit. "Arrogance dismisses the long-standing foundation of the church!" he said, calling the service to a close.

But the congregation was moved.

"Some preachers chop at the branches of the popish heresy, but Knox strikes at the root!" said one man to Rough as he exited the church.

An old man behind him agreed. "Even George Wishart never spoke so well."

Rough nodded, amazed. "In one hour Knox has put more life in us than five hundred trumpets blasting continually," he told the boys. "Truly, he is the trumpeter of God."

That day Knox finally admitted that Rough was right in

calling him to the ministry. He kept teaching the boys, but he also started working with Rough. For months they held debates, wrote pamphlets promoting the Reformation, and held Protestant communion services. Knox's preaching drew bigger and bigger crowds. "At this rate, you'll convert all of St. Andrews in a year!" predicated Alexander.

But with the end of the summer came the end of the truce. The queen regent, tired of waiting on the governor, called on her allies in France. George and Francis were among the first to look out the North Tower and see the French ships anchored just beyond the cliffs, their canons aimed at the castle.

Messengers were dispatched to England, asking again for aid. The drawbridge was hoisted. The iron gate was lowered. Soldiers rolled the cardinal's supply of canon balls into place up on the battlements.

The castle was under siege.

It wasn't long before supplies began to run low and some of the people fell sick.

Knox called an emergency meeting. From his chapel pulpit, he delivered a warning to the castle garrison. "Our situation here has taken a turn for the worse. You have dealt deceitfully with the governor. You have lived like pagans. You put your hope for salvation in the English, rather than God. Now disease is spreading among you and food is running out. I call you to repent! Repent while there is time——."

But his words were cut off by an explosion.

"The French are firing on us!" Leslie cried. "To your posts, men!"

They scattered to the defenses. A second volley of canon fire burrowed into the castle walls.

"My students!" was Knox's urgent thought. He had left them in the library taking a grammar lesson from Alexander when he called his hasty meeting with the garrison.

He stumbled out of the pulpit, the floor trembling beneath his feet. Shoving past the heavy doors, he ran outside and into a cloud of smoke. It choked him and stung his eyes. Soldiers rushed past him in the haze, shouting orders. He tried to work his way through the chaos toward the central buildings. He still had his two-handed sword in his room. It was too heavy to carry all the time. But now he had to find it and get to his students.

The earth rumbled again and threw him to the ground. Chunks of stone rained down around him. He pushed himself up, set his sights on the doorway ahead, and made a dash for it.

Inside, the booming of the canons was more muffled. But a thunderous blast from the other direction told him the castle garrison was returning fire now. He raced into his room, where smoke was curling in the window. Yanking the sword from the wall with both hands, he darted out again.

"Master Knox!" shouted Alexander when the teacher burst into the library. Half a dozen students were huddled together along the central wall.

"Good, you're safe!" Knox said, rushing to them.

George turned a white face to his tutor. "We're ready to fight, Master! Tell us what to do."

Knox shook his dust-covered head and gathered the boys around him. "Nay, nay. Alexander is right in keeping you here. This side of the castle is safest from the canons. If we can keep the walls from falling in on us, we'll survive." He glanced at the ceiling. "This battle will not last long, I'm afraid."

He was right. The barrage continued all night. But around daybreak, the canons fell quiet. A long blast of a trumpet sounded a cease fire. The battle was over. The Reformed lords had surrendered to the governor and his French mercenaries.

Twelve years later, Knox faced the crumbling castle with Lord James at his side and 3000 Lords of the Congregation behind him.

"Master Knox?" prompted Lord James. "Are you ill?"

Knox looked startled. "What?"

"You were telling me about the battle here when you suddenly fell quiet. Do you need to rest?"

"No, I'm sorry. It's just that seeing these towers again reminds me of George Wishart." Knox was still staring at the remains of the castle.

The young man took the preacher's arm and gently urged him forward again. "We're almost to the city, Master Knox. Please finish the story. What happened after the garrison surrendered? Is that when you were captured?"

Knox tugged at his beard. "Aye. We were all captured, all of us who survived. My pupils eventually made it back to their homes. But Leslie and Kirkcaldy and I and all the responsible lairds were convicted of treason. I was one of many prisoners traded to the French navy as payment for their assistance. For two years I was a slave in the galley of one of their ships. The commander was a godless man who beat us for nothing and pushed us to labor far more than our bodies could take." He pointed his walking stick at his knee. "That's why my limbs are so damaged today."

James nodded in sympathy. "But the English government negotiated for your release."

"Sometimes it pays to have high-ranking friends," Knox agreed. "Once I was released, I spent some years in England assisting in the Reformation there. That is what convinces me that all of this was God's will. If I had not been captured, I never would have left Scotland. And if I never had left Scotland, I never would have met Master Calvin in Geneva and learned from him just how much a state might be changed for the glory of Christ!"

"And here we are on our way to St. Andrews to do just that," said Lord James with a grand sweep of his arm toward the city. "The fact that the queen has outlawed Protestant preachers means she knows just how much influence you have."

"I won't stop preaching until I'm in the grave—and even then I make no promises!" He laughed, but his eyes took on a faraway look again. "If only Wishart was with us today to see what the Lord has done in his beloved Scotland."

"He would give you much of the credit, as do I. The Reformed cause would not have prospered without the preaching of the Trumpeter of God!"

"Well, this trumpet has at least one long blast left in him, my lord. Just get me to the church."

"Aye. It is a privilege, Master Knox!" declared Lord James.

An army of Scottish lords delivered the trumpet back to the pulpit of St. Andrews.

Upon his arrival in St. Andrews and under the protection of the army, Knox began preaching again in the old parish church. Knox's preaching at St. Andrews convinced more leaders to take up the cause of the Reformation. In 1560, when the queen regent died, the lords formed a Protestant Parliament. Knox helped draft the First Book of Discipline *and the* Scottish Confession of Faith. *He is most famous for writing his* History of the Reformation in Scotland *and remains to this day one of the most important figures in Scottish church history. Knox and his first wife, Marjory, had two boys. She died in December of 1560. In 1563 he married Margaret Stewart, a relative of Queen Mary. They had three daughters. He died in 1572.*

Little is known about his pupils, but we do know that Alexander became a respected scholar and author.

WAR AND RELIGION

WHY IS IT that in the long history of the world, the combination of religion and politics has often led to war?

One reason is because people identify themselves and their nation partly by their religion. To preserve their national heritage, they impose their religion upon others. They see how God has blessed their nation and they believe his blessing is a reward for their obedience. So they think rejecting the national religion risks God's displeasure. They might even outlaw the freedom of other religious groups to protect the majority.

Another reason is because people who have no freedom to worship want that freedom desperately. They are willing to fight against their leaders to force them to tolerate their beliefs.

Sometimes people wage war to overturn the official religion of the state, hoping to make their religion the national religion.

Since the time of Constantine, Christianity has been an official religion of many nations. During the time of the Reformation it was no different. During the Crusades of the medieval period, the fighting was mostly between Christians and Muslims. During the Reformation, the fighting was between Christians of different stripes: Catholics vs. Protestants or, sometimes, Protestants vs. Protestants who were slightly different.

In Germany, for example, *Lutheranism* gave the people a national cause. The princes took the opportunity to free themselves from the control of both the Roman church and Holy Roman Emperor Charles V. Starting in February 1531, several German princes formed the *Schmalkaldic League* to protect the religious freedoms of German rulers. The League was defeated by Charles in 1547, but when Henry II of France agreed to help the League in exchange for land, Charles was in turn defeated. His empire was turned over to his brother Ferdinand, who managed to secure the Peace of Augsburg in 1555. That agreement said the people would follow the religion of their ruler (Catholic or Lutheran), and those who did not agree were allowed to sell their land and move. The strong religious reasons for this struggle are clear from the many attempts to find common ground between Catholics and Protestants on biblical teaching. One of these attempts is the Lutheran statement of faith called the *Augsburg Confession*, written in 1530.

In France, the search for religious freedom led to clashes between Calvinist Huguenots and the Catholic royalty. France was divided by three powerful families: the Guises, the Châtillons, and the Bourbons. The Guises were dedicated Catholics. They clashed with the queen mother Catherine de Medici, who ruled as regent for her young sons Charles and Henry. Early in her rule, Catherine, who was also Catholic, formed an alliance against the Guises with the Huguenot Châtillon and Bourbon families. But by the mid-1560s, she clashed with Huguenot leaders and revoked her practice of toleration. The Huguenot armies rallied to fight for the freedom to worship as Calvinists. Several short-lived peace agreements led to a string of wars between Protestants and Catholics known as the

Wars of Religion. Those wars finally came to an end with the Edict of Nantes in 1598. This peace agreement allowed for limited freedoms of the Huguenots and lasted until 1685, when it was revoked by Louis XIV in the Edict of Fontainebleau. The Huguenots lost their freedoms and fled from France.

At times, the religious motives for war are nearly impossible to separate from the political ones. For example, by 1618, the *Thirty Years' War* spilled over national boundaries involving all of Central Europe. The war involved alliances between Protestants and Catholics and a conflict between France and Spain, both Catholic countries. Religious motives were certainly important for then Holy Roman Emperor Ferdinand II, a strong supporter of the Counter Reformation. He imposed the Edict of Restitution, an act that restored church property in Protestant territory to the Catholic Church. The Thirty Years' War ended with the Peace of Westphalia on October 24, 1648. From that peace, religious minorities were given certain freedoms and Calvinists were recognized.

Religion is just one reason among many why people go to war. Sometimes the dominant reasons are not religion, but money, politics, or just plain hatred of other people. But one thing is for sure—every war is as complicated as the people fighting it!

Jeanne d'Albret: Deborah of the Huguenots

MARCH 1569. JARNAC, FRANCE.

NOT FAR FROM COGNAC, cannonballs screeched through the sky, blasting holes in the earth. Smoke drifted into the woods, making the men darting between the trees look like ghosts. Gunfire crackled, and two horses crumpled, throwing their riders to the ground with shrieking neighs.

"Forward! Forward!" bellowed a fallen horseman. Grasping his right thigh, he stumbled back against a tree. The smell of gunpowder burned his nostrils.

A rider approached. "A message for Prince Louis de Bourbon de Condé!"

"Over here."

The boy slid off his saddle, brandishing a sealed letter. "It's from Admiral Coligny."

Prince Condé pulled the boy behind the tree and broke the wax seal. "Coligny and his men are outnumbered near the abbey in Bassac," he shouted to his lieutenant, crouched behind another clump of trees. "They are near defeat and need more men."

"To get to Coligny we'd have to break through Anjou's ranks," the lieutenant shouted back.

"If Queen Jeanne will not surrender to the royalists, neither shall we!" He swung the boy back up on his horse, but did not release the iron grip on his arm. "We are fighting for the freedom of the Huguenots to worship according to their conscience," he reminded the boy with urgency. "We must not back away from this fight. Do you understand me?"

"Yes, Prince."

"Good. Fall back to the flank and get as many knights as you can to follow me. Now!"

The boy leaned into his horse's neck and flew off into the trees.

Condé ran, crouching, to his lieutenant. "I am a Bourbon. Let no one say that a Bourbon fled before his enemies!" he said, a hard glitter in his eyes. "Find us more horses!"

A thunderous pounding of hooves announced that Condé and his knights were storming the field. As they approached Anjou's position, eight hundred pairs of eyes took aim.

"Charge!" shouted Condé. Clanging steel and pistol shots rang through the air. The prince's horse galloped headlong into the enemy army, his rider swinging his sword in a wide arc.

Behind him, the Huguenot knights fell, one after the other.

Within minutes he was surrounded by royalists. He fought valiantly, until a gun crackled and his horse collapsed to the ground on top of him.

A knight from Anjou's army dismounted. "Are you Prince Condé?" he demanded.

He raised the visor of his helmet with his free hand, breathing heavily under the weight of his beast. "It is I," he gasped.

"I served under you when you served King Francis," said the knight, freeing him from his horse. "Your life will be spared."

"Your kindness reflects Christ." He took the knight's outstretched hand and gritted his teeth as he raised himself on one foot. "I'm afraid my leg is broken."

"I'll take you to Anjou to discuss your surrender." He glanced across the field.

Condé followed his gaze. Henry Anjou, younger brother of France's King Charles and son of the Queen Mother Catherine de Medici, sat atop his horse. He was talking with Marshall Cossé, general of the royalist forces.

When Anjou saw Condé, he pointed. Cossé barked an order. The captain of Anjou's army jerked his reigns, charged toward them, and drew his pistol.

"No!" shouted the knight supporting Condé.

But a single shot rang out, and the Huguenot prince collapsed.

"What have you done?" cried the knight. "He surrendered! I offered him his life!"

"Anjou's orders," declared the captain, and galloped away.

Anjou and Cossé turned their horses and followed the captain, joined by the surviving troops. The knight stared at Condé's body.

As the smoke cleared, he saw dozens of men strewn across the battlefield. Some wore the colors of the Protestant Huguenots. Others wore the colors of the Catholic royalists. They were all French, dead at the hands of their brothers.

A few days later, a ship bearing the arms of Admiral Gaspard de Coligny, of the House of Châtillon, sailed into the harbor of La Rochelle. The city was built right on the harbor, with a tall white tower guarding both sides of the waterway. Canons protruded from the tower windows. Banners with Queen Jeanne's insignia flew from the fortifications.

At the ship's prow stood the last surviving leader of the Huguenot army. Gaspard de Coligny was dressed in black except for the red and gold on his chest armor. His beard was streaked with gray, and damp from the spray of the boat as they sailed between the two towers and docked in the harbor.

Disembarking, Coligny and his guards were swiftly escorted into the castle courtyard. A tall, well-dressed man stood ready to greet them.

"Monsieur Etienne!" said Coligny, with a military bow. "Good to see you again."

"And you, my friend. Come right in."

Coligny followed him through the arch and up a wide staircase. "Is the queen keeping you out of trouble?"

"What good would a dead secretary be?" There was a trace of sarcasm in his voice, but he was too serious to smile.

They passed a pair of armed guards and entered a large chamber. Floor-to-ceiling windows overlooked the harbor. The setting sun pierced the glass, and Coligny was dazzled by the sudden reflection on the marble floors. He averted his eyes, and there to his left was the woman he had come to see.

Etienne bowed. "The Queen of Navarre and the Huguenots, Jeanne d'Albret," he announced.

Coligny and his men dropped to their knees before her.

"Welcome, Gaspard," said the queen softly.

He raised his head and looked at her with respect. She had deep-set eyes and a long nose. The curls pulled back under her close-fitting veil showed signs of gray. She had worn black every day since her husband Antoine de Bourbon was killed in battle. Today, the black gown was adorned with a high, ruffled collar and a double strand of pearls that hung to her waist.

She stretched out her arm to him. "Rise, and walk with me."

He took his place at her side as she paced the room.

"What a tragic defeat we have suffered," Jeanne said, twisting a small lace handkerchief in her hands. "Condé's death is a loss to the House of Bourbon and to the Huguenots. My only consolation is that he died with honor in the service of his God."

He nodded solemnly. "The prince was a brave warrior and a fine man."

"Is it true that Anjou shot him in cold blood after he had surrendered?"

"I'm afraid so. Anjou has no honor, to betray a prince in such a manner!"

"I thank God that you survived, Gaspard. We would be forsaken if you had been lost as well."

"Spared for the battle ahead, no doubt."

She began to cough, a sudden spasm from deep in her chest. She turned away from him, a hand over her mouth, until the fit had passed. When she turned back, he noticed flecks of blood on her handkerchief.

"Your health has not improved, my queen?"

The effort had drawn tears to her eyes. She dabbed at them with a finger. "No, my cough grows worse each day. But there is no point in dwelling on that. You, Gaspard, are now the sole leader of the Huguenot military. We must develop a new strategy."

"The military is not strong at the moment," he admitted. "After Jarnac, I'm afraid we must recruit all over again. The common people do not believe they have a right to resist their rulers, so they will not fight on our behalf without support of the royalty."

"I know," she agreed. "That is why my son Henry, as well as Condé's son, will lead the military under you."

"They are mere youths, my queen. They have very little experience in leading an army."

"Henry is seventeen and like his father in many ways," she reminded him. "He will excel with your training."

He bowed. "If that is your wish."

"But I have not given up on diplomacy, Gaspard. I shall write again to Catherine de Medici." She paused, as though she might cough again. But she continued. "We are fighting for the freedom of French Calvinists to worship according to their consciences. I must convince the queen mother and her son that it is not worth this bloodshed to force us into submission to the church of Rome."

"I am a warrior," he said. "But given our current loss at Jarnac, I believe you are wise to try negotiating again. You have already proven that you have no desire to suppress religion in your realm. Perhaps she will be willing to do the same."

"Remember Theodore Beza, who preached in my court for three months?" When he nodded, she continued. "I have been writing to him and, as usual, his advice is indispensable. He has contacted Catherine on our behalf. He has even gone so far as to remind her that though the Reformed smash Catholic images, we do not order the hanging of men!"

Coligny closed his eyes, remembering the massacre at Vassy. Catherine de Medici refused to allow the Huguenots to worship in the churches, but she finally promised them the right to worship freely in barns outside the city limits. But when her soldiers came upon twelve hundred Huguenots worshipping just outside Vassy, they started a riot that led to the slaughter of nearly all the worshippers.

"I do not wish my son to become such a ruler, Admiral," she said with determination.

He looked her in the eye. "I will train him with integrity."

Servants came in to light the candelabras. Jeanne put a hand on Coligny's arm and took another turn around the room. "I have also sent messengers to Queen Elizabeth in England. We are appealing to her for military aid."

"She has been hesitant to get involved in our civil war."

"But the Reformation in England has grown under her leadership. And she did assist the Protestants in Scotland. Perhaps she will do the same for France. I can only hope that the examples set by her stepmother Queen Katherine Parr and her brother King Edward will keep her dedicated to the Reformed cause."

She began to cough again, and he stayed at her side. When she stopped, her face was white and beads of perspiration clung to her forehead.

"Gather the troops, Admiral," she said in a hoarse voice. "I will talk to Henry, and we will address the army when you are ready."

He bowed over her gloved hand.

"We are like the Israelites," Jeanne reminded him as he turned away. "God will deliver us into the promised land where we can worship freely."

Etienne led the soldiers away, and Jeanne went to speak to her son.

The doors in Henry's parlor were open, the satin draperies billowing out onto the balcony. She found him out there in the dark, his face toward the sea.

"The admiral has returned," he said, without turning around. "What happens next?"

"You will lead the military with Coligny and his men," she answered from the doorway.

"So you are willing to let me go, then?" Henry asked.

"As a mother, I wish you would remain here in safety. But as a queen, I must prepare you to rule. Our people need you to lead them to freedom."

The wind blew the curls back from his forehead as he nodded. She went to his side and ran a hand through his hair.

"Trust in God's providence, my son," she said, grateful that the darkness hid her tears. "You are ready for this. Coligny is waiting for you." She left him with a kiss on his cheek.

Coligny and Henry went right to work, recruiting and training a new army. Queen Jeanne left La Rochelle to meet them at their camp. They stood at attention before her, their armor dull and their eyes heavy.

"The Reformed religion is not dead," she proclaimed, "just as our God is not dead."

They murmured their agreement.

"No, my friends. Hear me. Our God is not dead!" she shouted. "And the courage of those following him should never fail. He has chosen you for a brave mission, and he will not forsake you."

The weary soldiers began to cheer. Jeanne put a hand on her son's shoulder. "Henry is a prince of the blood. He can rightfully lead you brave men to your freedom."

A chant of "Henry! Henry!" went up.

Henry stepped forward. "I am a Huguenot," he called, raising his sword high. "I swear never to abandon our religion. I call upon you to do the same. Will you fight for the freedom of our people?"

The army shouted their allegiance.

Admiral Coligny turned to Jeanne. "It appears they are ready to follow Henry."

"As he follows you," said Jeanne. "I'm going back to La Rochelle to negotiate for our peace or find more men to fight. You have your orders."

He held her gaze. "Yes, Madam General, and I have an order for you: rest. We rely on your strength."

She gave him a grim smile. "God be with you, Admiral."

It was late when she arrived back at the city.

"You look exhausted, my queen," Etienne said as he met her carriage.

"Travel tightens my lungs," she admitted to her secretary, loosening her collar. "I must go to bed now. Bring me an update first thing in the morning."

"Of course."

"I expect we are to suffer many more losses before this is over," she murmured, and left him at the door of her apartment.

She went to bed, but her mind was too troubled to sleep. She prayed most of the night, and sent for her secretary just after dawn. Etienne arrived at her sitting room with news.

"Coligny sends word that he is on his way to Moncontour as ordered, Your Grace. We just received and decoded his dispatch."

"Very well."

"And there is more," he said with a look of relief. "We have secured some German mercenaries, and Queen Elizabeth has delivered supplies of gunpowder and canons from England."

"Excellent, Etienne." She drew her shawl more closely around her shoulders. "Now is the right time to send another appeal to Paris. As I tried to sleep, a letter was taking shape in my mind."

He went to her desk and prepared a sheet of paper and a jar of ink. The words flowed from his careful hand as she dictated them:

To the Illustrious Queen Mother Catherine: As I have before, I write to you again. You have not responded to our demands for freedom to worship according to our consciences and according to Scripture. I cannot believe you would want us to have no religion! So much blood has been shed already. You can stop the bloodshed with just a word. I implore you to make peace.

She signed the letter herself, and watched as Etienne sealed it with wax.

"I will send this immediately." He gave her a concerned look. "Have you eaten this morning?"

"Not yet."

He called for a chambermaid, who appeared instantly. "Send up the queen's breakfast."

"Send it to the war room," Jeanne corrected. "I have work to do." She began to rise, but a fit of coughing overcame her.

"Your health grows worse," he said.

She leaned back in her chair, exhausted. "I try not to think about it," she said. "I fear that if I die, the Huguenot army will fall apart and our cause will be lost."

He gave her a rare smile. "You are the Deborah of the Huguenots, like the ancient judge of Israel who led her people to victory. I believe you will secure peace in France before you are taken to your eternal rest."

"Thank you, Etienne. I pray that you are right. Now, go, dispatch messengers with that letter. I'll meet you in the war room shortly."

The war room was a large parlor Jeanne had converted into her military headquarters. Decorative tapestries and mirrors still hung from the walls, but the queen had removed all the furniture to make room for four large tables. They were covered with maps. Her aids flitted about, decoding messages, marking troop movements, and writing up rosters and receipts for supplies.

Jeanne spent all her waking hours in the war room, with Etienne at her side. She dispatched orders to Coligny. She wrote letters to kings and cardinals, asking them to support a peace treaty. She hired pirates to storm French ships and capture their canons. She sent tax collectors into her territories to raise funds for more armor.

Every night in her dreams, Henry called out to her from the battlefield. She would awake, coughing, then fall back on the pillows, gasping, when it was over. When the coughing was really bad, her chest hurt so much she could not go back to sleep. Instead, she spent the night staring up at the lacy bed curtains and blotting the sweat from her brow.

One afternoon, the door burst open on the war room and the guards escorted in a soldier who fell before the queen and thrust out a sealed message. Etienne ripped it open.

"It's Coligny," he said, scanning the document. "He's been defeated at Moncontour and he's withdrawing the troops. He was shot in the face, but he survived and needs your orders."

"There was a tremendous slaughter," said the messenger, rising. "But Prince Henry wanted you to know he is safe."

"Thank God!" She turned to an aid. "Get this soldier water and a fresh horse."

The young man scurried out to obey. The rest of her aids clustered around her as she hunched over one of the map tables.

"Where were you last?" she asked the messenger.

"Coligny ordered troops south toward Languedoc."

"Here." She put her finger on the map. "Good."

She began to draw out routes on the map, and debated with

her advisors. One aid began to take down her message as another transferred it into code.

She pressed her seal into the hot wax and thrust the envelope into the messenger's hands. "See that these orders make it back to Coligny."

He was moving out the door even as he bowed.

Jeanne collapsed in a chair, her hands over her face. Etienne leaned over her with a whisper.

"They say there is a bounty on Coligny's head, Your Grace."

"A bounty!"

"If he gets captured, they won't trade him for one of our hostages as they have done in the past. They'll just kill him like they did Condé."

She shook her head. "They have tried to assassinate me. My son is on the front lines. And now they have placed a bounty on the admiral's head. It is too much, Etienne."

"It is more than anyone should have to bear, and your health is already weak. Why don't you lie down for a few hours? Your orders have been sent. We will hear nothing more today."

"You're right," she said, rising. "We will know more tomorrow, because I am going to visit the troops myself."

Her aids looked up at her, startled, from their positions around the map tables.

Etienne's heavy eyebrows shot up. "My queen?"

"Ready a military escort, and prepare to deliver gunpowder and any other supplies they need," she ordered, collecting her black shawl from the back of a chair. "I want to meet with the troops personally."

"Are you sure it is wise to leave La Rochelle?"

"If I wasn't sure, I would not have given the order," she said sternly. "I sent these men to fight for their religion. It is only right that I support them. Make preparations. I shall leave at dawn."

She swept out of the room regally, but before the double doors closed behind her, they could hear her anguished cough echoing in the corridor.

Her caravan set out the next morning. She left La Rochelle in Etienne's charge. Knights hurried ahead of her carriage, waving her banner. Several of her aids and a nurse rode with her. Behind them followed several wagons loaded with barrels of gunpowder, crates of biscuits, and several dozen pistols.

When she arrived at the camp, Coligny was waiting for her outside his tent. A bandage covered one side of his face, and his arm was wrapped in a sling.

"My queen, this is unexpected! It is not safe for you to leave La Rochelle."

She looked out the carriage window at him. "It is no safer for you. I will not be cooped up in the city while my men are dying!"

"The men do not doubt your convictions, Jeanne."

She stepped out of the carriage, and took in the row of soldiers standing at attention behind the admiral. Their faces were black with gunpowder and some were missing pieces of their armor. But the sight of their queen set their eyes shining.

"This war is hard on everyone, Gaspard," she said, turning back to him. "I am not ignorant of the sacrifices these men have made. I am here to remind them of our cause, to encourage them to persevere."

A general strode toward them in black armor like the admiral's. It took her a moment to realize it was Henry. He had grown a narrow mustache and was thinner than when she had last seen him. It had been only a few weeks, but he seemed years older.

She resisted the urge to throw her arms around him. "It is good to see you alive, my son!"

"I know you like to get involved, Mother, but surely you have not come to take up arms with us!"

"I'm here to remind you of the cause," said Jeanne. "This may seem like an inevitable failure, but I am confident we will prevail.

We must stay the course."

"Your timing is uncanny," said the admiral, drawing close. "I was about to dispatch a messenger to you. I have a plan that may gain us the upper hand."

"Tell me!"

Henry pulled aside the tent flap and the three of them went in. The queen's knights immediately formed a circle around the tent, arms drawn.

Inside, Coligny pulled up a stool for the queen with his good arm. "Anjou's army did not follow us from Moncontour as I expected," he explained. "So clearly he has some other plan which I intend to discover. In the meantime, I need to gather more soldiers and give Charles and Catherine in Paris a reason to negotiate for peace."

"What do you have in mind?" demanded Jeanne.

"We plan on getting our men all the way to the king's courtyard!" said Henry. "We can fortify ourselves within forty miles of Paris, but it's going to take patience and a diversion."

"What kind of diversion?"

"Anjou is greedy for winning battles that bring him fame, right?" said Coligny, leaning against a table. "He's not interested in simply killing the rest of my battered army. So we'll continue to move through the south, regrouping with the rest of our men stationed there."

Jeanne's brow creased with a frown. "That will leave La Rochelle and other cities nearly unprotected!"

"Indeed," agreed Coligny. "But Anjou will not go directly to La Rochelle. St. Jean d'Angély is closer and a victory there would be a boost for his cause. When he sees that we have withdrawn our protection, he will start there."

"She is a well-fortified city," jumped in Henry, "and can withstand a siege for awhile."

Coligny nodded. "While Anjou is busy with this distraction, we will follow the River Rhône northwards to Arnay le Duc."

"And then he will discover that we have come between him and Paris!" said Jeanne, understanding. "But, Gaspard, you are putting all our eggs in one basket."

"An ambitious, well-planned basket," replied Coligny. Hindered by the bandage across his cheek, his bearded smile looked sinister. "It is all we have."

Jeanne took a deep breath. "Then we must try it. I will maintain a few smaller armies nearby and send for reinforcements at La Rochelle. We can only hope we have guessed Anjou's actions correctly." She rose. "Assemble the troops, Admiral. I intend to address them before I leave here."

The queen returned to La Rochelle that evening. She went back to writing letters during the day and praying for victory during the night. But her heart was on the battlefield with her son, the admiral, and the Huguenot troops they commanded.

The following days proved Admiral Coligny's strategy wise. As expected, Anjou abandoned his pursuit of the Huguenot army and laid siege to St. Jean d'Angély. The city had a strong garrison and fought back. The damages to the royalist army were so great, Anjou left them in the hands of General Cossé and went back to Paris to sulk. The Huguenots had fled to the south anyway, he thought.

But Coligny had been picking up troops in the south and began to sneak north along the Rhône. When the news reached Cossé, he knew it could mean only one thing: Coligny and the Huguenots were marching on Paris! Cossé pulled his troops away from St. Jean d'Angély in pursuit.

The two battle-weary armies met on the hills of Arnay, outside Paris. With cries of "Charge!" they raced down both sides of the valley toward the stream at the bottom.

Canon blasts and the clash of swords echoed in the hills.

When darkness fell, both sides retreated to their camps to count their losses. Coligny galloped up to a stand of trees, where Henry was on his knees helping treat the wounds of his men.

"It is good to see you alive, young prince!"

"My mother wouldn't have it any other way," said Henry, wiping his hands on his trousers and joining the admiral at his horse.

"She has been praying today," nodded Coligny. "I can feel it." His bandages were gone now. But his arm was still weak, and his beard did not cover the scar on his cheek. He counted the campfires on the other side of the valley. "It looks like Cossé has suffered more than we have."

"He's wishing he had finished us off after Moncontour! Now it is our turn."

Coligny shook his head. "No. Our goal is to force peace, not kill every last royalist. La Charité is only a short distance from here and they are friendly to Protestants. If we can make it there and fortify ourselves in this region, Paris will be forced to finally acknowledge the Huguenots."

"Cossé is not going to just let us march into La Charité. We'll have to trick him again."

"Exactly." Coligny leaned in closer. "We leave our camp set up here, and tomorrow the first wave, under my command, will line up along the ridge as he expects. He will look for another chance to test our strength. While we are engaged, you will lead the remainder of our men to La Charité. The residents will see Jeanne's banners and open the gates to you. The battle will be over."

"We'll begin preparations now, Admiral." Henry mounted his horse.

"Excellent. And Henry…"

The prince wheeled his animal around. "Yes, Admiral."

"You have proven to be as worthy a leader as your mother said. I'm proud to serve with the future King of Navarre."

Henry beamed at him, and urged his horse toward the camp.

That night, Jeanne lay in her bed and prayed until well after the candles had burned out.

When the sun rose over the valley, Coligny and one of his

regiments were poised for battle on the hill. With the blast of a horn, the royalist troops rushed toward them, desperate to gain the upper hand right away.

But Cossé soon realized that something was wrong. "There are not enough troops out there!" he cried to his lieutenant. "And their camp is empty! Where are they?"

"The flank is clear, Sir. The only movements are in front of us," insisted the confused soldier.

Cossé sucked in his breath. "La Charité! They're making a run to the city! Order the troops to fall back and go after them!"

Coligny knew the ruse was up. "Retreat!" he cried, standing in his saddle. "On to the city, men!" He could only hope that Henry and his men had made it there safely.

The Huguenots turned their horses and galloped toward La Charité, with Cossé's army hot on their trail. It was miles to the city. They leaned forward in their saddles, the foam flying off the horses. Pistol shots rang out behind them. Some of the horses fell.

"Forward!" Coligny urged his troops. "Faster!"

The walls of La Charité came into view and grew larger as they flew toward the city.

"The gates are open!" came the cry. "Henry made it!"

"Go! Go!" Coligny shouted.

Canon fire erupted from the city and sent Cossé's cavalry scattering. With the smoke behind them, Coligny and his men crossed the remaining distance and pounded through the gates.

Henry's men were waiting for them with a cheer. The prince grasped Coligny's hand and swung him down from the saddle. He was grinning from ear to ear. "We can wave to Paris from here!" he shouted above the clamor.

Far away, in the fortress of La Rochelle, the queen of Navarre knelt in her chapel. She was so intent on her prayers, she did not hear Etienne's approaching footsteps. He knelt beside her.

"You have news?" She looked up with anxious eyes.

He smiled at her. "Your patience has paid off, Jeanne. Coligny has given Catherine and Charles something to fear. He's established himself near Paris."

She clutched at her pearls with relief. "Our God is merciful!"

"Our troops are at La Charité. The royalist forces are so devastated, they've called a truce. And word has arrived that a letter from Paris is on the way. Catherine is ready to work toward peace."

"And Henry?"

"He's fine."

She began to rise, but severe coughing brought her to her knees again. She pressed her handkerchief to her mouth and forced herself to breathe slowly. "I did not think I would live to see peace," she whispered.

He helped her to her feet. "With Coligny's courage and your conviction, the Reformed faith has won a great victory!"

"In God's providence," she said. "Let us pray for a lasting peace."

Leaning on her secretary, the frail queen headed to the war room to prepare a peace treaty.

In August 1570, an edict of peace was signed at St. Germain. Believing it would seal a peace, Jeanne gave her blessing to her son's marriage to Catherine de Medici's daughter, Marguerite. But Jeanne missed the wedding. On June 9, 1572, with Coligny at her bedside, she died of tuberculosis at the age of forty-four. Henry was married on August 18. Six days later, by order of King Charles IX, thousands of Huguenots were slaughtered and their leaders assassinated in the Saint Bartholomew's Day Massacre.

After Charles's death, Henry of Navarre became King Henry IV of France, but struggled to maintain the peace between Catholics and Protestants. He eventually concluded that the only way to avoid more bloodshed was for him to become Catholic. In the spirit of his mother, he signed the Edict of Nantes, which ended the French Wars of Religion.

Jeanne of Navarre is said to be the only sovereign of the sixteenth century who never put anyone to death for religion.

THE SETTLING OF THE AMERICAS

FOR EUROPEANS DURING the Renaissance and Reformation, the world became suddenly bigger with the discovery of the Americas. The famous explorer Christopher Columbus was not the first European to come to the Americas. In the year 1000, Leif Ericson of Norway discovered what is today called Newfoundland in North America. But Columbus's landing on October 12, 1492, and his later voyages opened the gate for further exploration and eventual colonization.

Other adventurers—many of them from Spain—soon followed. In 1513, Juan Ponce de León searched for an island which was said to be the location of a "fountain of youth." What he found instead is present-day Florida. Hernando Cortés (1485-1547) also journeyed to find rumored treasure and magical cities, only to discover the Aztec people of Mexico. In 1540, Francisco Vásquez de Coronado set out on an expedition for the Seven Cities of Gold. His search for the legend sent him exploring as far as Kansas, but he came back empty-handed.

Stories of adventure in foreign lands circulated throughout Europe. Each year, more explorers braved the seas. Several attempts to plant colonies in the New World were made by French, English, and Dutch settlers. Some of these, like the Roanoke Island colony (1590) failed. Others, like Jamestown (1607), laid the foundation for future settlements.

Many made the trip not for gold or land, but just to start their lives over or find religious freedom. In 1620, Captain Christopher Jones of the *Mayflower* brought a small separatist congregation led by William Brewster and William Bradford to Plymouth. Their settlement was the beginning of the Massachusetts Bay Colony. After 1630, English Puritans and others began flooding to the Massachusetts Bay.

Both Protestant and Catholic missionaries set out to convert the native people of the new land. Historians do not agree about how to interpret these efforts. Some say the missionaries were just tools for their governments to oppress the Indians. Others say the Indians knew they had much to gain from cooperating with the colonists. The truth is somewhere in the middle. The Indians and the Europeans were all human beings, so they had both good and bad motives. No doubt some of the Indian conversions were forced and some were genuine. Disputes arose between the colonists and the Indians because of mistakes, misunderstandings, and deceptions on both sides. This was especially true of *King Philip's War* (1675-1676), a bloody confrontation between a Wampanoag chieftain and English settlers in Massachusetts Bay.

But many Christians did have a genuine desire to bring the gospel to the new land. Missionaries like John Eliot and Daniel Gookin were successful among the Indians. Like others of his day, Eliot did not approve of the way Indians dressed and wore their hair, and he insisted that the Christian Indians reflect European lifestyles as much as possible. But he also spent over forty years riding on horseback from one Indian town to the next, preaching the Bible to them and training native pastors. He developed the Algonquian speech into a written language and then translated the whole Bible and taught them to read it. He believed the Indians should govern themselves through trained leaders, and he defended Christian and non-Christian Indians from those who wanted to sell them into slavery. His methods set the standard for missions of the next century.

The Protestant English colonies grew. With the Woollens Acts of 1698 and the Test Act of 1672, a large number of Scottish Presbyterians from the Ulster colony in Ireland would also make their way to America. Reformation theology would have a big influence in the settling of the New World.

WILLIAM BRADFORD: STRANGERS AND PILGRIMS

OCTOBER 1620. ABOARD THE MAYFLOWER, SOMEWHERE IN THE ATLANTIC OCEAN.

ONE HUNDRED MEN, women, and children were rolled into their hammocks in the great cabin below decks. They gripped the ropes with white knuckles as the ship rose and fell in the stormy seas. All around them in the dimness the wooden planks creaked under the strain. Cold seawater poured through gaps in the ceiling, soaking their clothes. Most of the hanging lanterns had been snuffed out, and now swung from the beams like empty cages.

One man tried to lead the passengers in singing and prayer. He had to hunch his shoulders to stand under the low ceiling. "Take courage, friends. God did not bring us this far to kill us!" he shouted against the storm. "He will deliver us to a new life in Virginia!"

His white hair and beard stuck to his face in wet clumps. Letting go of a beam with one hand, he tried to wipe his forehead. Just then, the ship rolled hard to starboard. He stumbled and was smacked in the head by a table scudding across the wet floor.

"Oh!" the minister moaned, trying to find his footing. A thin line of blood trickled down his soggy whiskers.

"Mrs. Brewster, your husband is trying to preach away the storm again!" cried one of the passengers.

Mary Brewster left her children in the hammock. She made her way unsteadily to her husband and helped him back to the security of the ropes. As soon as they reached the hammock again, she pulled out a wet handkerchief and dabbed at his wound.

"Perhaps God is reminding you that Ecclesiastes says there is a time to be silent!" she said tenderly. "The congregation will appreciate your preaching better when they can hear it, my dear. Now look what you've done. You've ruined your last good collar."

Blood stained the wide square collar of his green jacket. But he glanced down at the snagged stockings below his knee breeches, and the missing buckle of one shoe.

"Ecclesiastes also says there is a time to throw away!" he pointed out.

A man in the next hammock chuckled. He was younger than Brewster, with a thin face and a neatly-trimmed mustache. "Maybe your next child should be named Silence," he suggested.

Mary twisted to face him. "Look here, William Bradford! Do you have a problem with our children's names?"

"Of course not," insisted Bradford. "Fear, Patience, Love, and Wrestling are lovely names. I am sure they will be quite fashionable in the New World."

He hoped his jokes would help ease the tension among the sick and frightened passengers. But the Brewsters braced themselves as another wave washed over the decks and splashed down above them.

Bradford glanced at his wife beside him. Her small frame was curled into a ball, and under her bonnet her eyes were red with crying. He reached an arm around her.

"Dorothy, it's all right," he said. "The storm won't last forever."

She shook her head. "It's not the storm! It's just—I look at the Brewster children all day, and I miss our little John."

"I miss our son, too," he said gently. "But he was too young and fragile to bring along on this trip. It is too dangerous."

She clung to him. "I know. But it's been two months!"

"We left him in good hands," he reminded her. "And we'll arrange his passage to the New World as soon as he's old enough to travel. We will all be together again."

She tried to blink back her tears, but they kept coming.

"As soon as this storm passes, we'll dry out our clothes and get some sleep," he promised. "We'll all feel better when the sun returns."

The ship rolled again and foamy seawater cascaded down the stairs like a waterfall.

"In the meantime, think of all the work we're saving," he said. "The fish are coming to us, instead of us having to catch them!"

She tried to smile through her tears.

The last of the lamps flickered out. A young man's voice cried, "That's it! I need air." Clatter sounded on the wet stairs as he headed above decks.

"You mustn't go up there, Howland! It's too dangerous!" shouted a man on the other side of the Bradfords. John Carver was bent over his sick wife. He sought out his friend in the darkness. "Bradford, would you be so kind as to go after him?"

Bradford left Dorothy in the hammock and scrambled toward the stairs. "Howland!"

The young man had reached the deck and was slipping and sliding toward the railing. The sails had been taken down, and the rigging smacked against the three bare masts in the wind. Rain fell in sheets, but at least the cold air out here didn't smell like sick people. He looked over the side. The wall of water rose and fell as the ship rocked.

"Get back to the cabin!" cried the sailor at the helm.

But the boy paid no attention.

"This is Captain Jones! I order you to return below!"

A wave crested, throwing the ship into another roll. Water rushed across the deck, carrying Howland over the railing. He was plunged into the water, but managed to grab on to one of the flying ropes.

Bradford burst out of the door just in time to see the captain sliding across the deck. The seaman snagged two posts with his feet and caught himself, hollering to his crew.

"Where's Howland?" Bradford shouted to the captain.

"Overboard!" was the reply.

He dashed to the railing after Captain Jones and spotted Howland's hand on the rope. "There he is!"

Jones leaned over and hauled the boy back onto deck with both hands. Howland's face was purple and he was shaking, but he was still breathing.

"Get him back down below! And keep him there!" the captain bellowed.

Bradford dragged the boy back toward the stairs. "No one but an experienced sailor should be up here!" he cried.

Howland jerked his arm away and struggled to navigate the stairs. "Who are you to tell me what to do? You're not much older than I am!"

"You're Carver's servant."

"I'm not his servant," replied the young man angrily. "I'm his assistant."

"Until you repay him the price of your passage, your duty is to him. You do not have the right to risk your life and the lives of others!" Bradford steered him back toward his hammock.

Howland fell into it, still coughing up seawater. When he looked up, his face was full of remorse. "You're right, Sir. I'm sorry."

Bradford hung onto the ropes and looked the boy in the eye. "You have as much a chance as anyone to make a good life in the colony, John Howland. You are strong and brave. You might even become a leader. But you have to make it there alive first!"

Dorothy gripped his hand as Bradford returned to their hammock. "What a foolish boy!" she said.

"The storm is making everyone crazy," he replied. "We must pray it will be over soon!"

Above the crashing of the waves, Bradford could hear Brewster humming psalms again.

Overnight, the storm began to subside. By sunrise, the waves had settled into a gentle rhythm and the rain had stopped, though dark clouds remained.

The captain warned that he didn't think the bad weather was over, but many of the passengers went above decks. The crew shouted at them for getting in the way. But everyone was happy at least to be on their feet and out in the dry salt air. They began to bail out the hold, where frying pans and candlesticks and saws for the new colony were floating in water.

On the main deck, Bradford was leaning over the railing where John Howland had nearly lost his life. The captain joined him there.

"How is the boy?"

"Fine," said Bradford. "Just ashamed of his foolishness. Thank you for your quick action, Captain."

Captain Jones leaned his elbows against the rail and looked up at the mainsail, which had been hoisted again. "Some folks aren't cut out for the sea. She makes them crazy."

"Count me among that number," declared Bradford.

"Well, the journey is nearly over."

"Getting off this ship is only the beginning. We have to build shelter and find food once we land."

"Others have done it," insisted the captain. "If most of you survive, you can build a fine society on the other side."

"I hope so," agreed Bradford. "Not all of the passengers are going for the same reasons we are. Brewster and I are working hard to convince the others to join our congregation. They do not agree with our religious convictions."

"You are separatists," said Jones.

"Some call us that, yes. There is little room for people like us in England. Holland was not a good option either. That's why we came to you in Leiden."

"How did you get there?"

"It took many years," said Bradford. "My parents died when I was a boy, and I was educated by a minister who disagreed with the Church of England. While I was there I met William Brewster, now the elder of our congregation. He taught me that the church must pursue purity."

"King James doesn't look fondly on those who refuse to conform," said Jones.

"That's why we had to leave England," Bradford explained. "We think it is wrong to kneel in worship, or for clergy to wear fancy robes. We believe we should not be forced to repeat a man-made liturgy. But James has imprisoned many separatist ministers just because they disagree with him about how Scripture tells us to worship."

"So you went to Holland?"

"We tried to charter a ship for Amsterdam. But her captain was a wicked man, and when we arrived at our secret meeting place, he robbed us and then turned us in to the authorities. Praise God they didn't find us to be worth their time! They let us go after we sat in prison for a long while." He paused. "Tell me why the king is more interested in imprisoning simple worshippers of God than he is in locking up the thieves and murderers?"

Jones grunted. "Some of those criminals have been on my ships, Bradford. The king promised them safe passage and a new life in Virginia if they were willing to go."

"Brewster has been thrown in prison several times and had to pay large fines to get out," said Bradford, shaking his head. "Another of our congregation had his face cut up, and was whipped for his beliefs! We eventually made it to Holland, and lived in Leiden for some time. But we realized we could no longer stay. The truce between the Dutch and the Spanish was almost over. And our children were forgetting their English heritage. That's why we came to you to take us to the New World."

"You are a man without a country," said the captain.

"We are strangers and pilgrims in this world," nodded Bradford. "We long for the day when we will enter our eternal home."

The ship's mate, a man called Clarke, shouted over to the captain.

"Well," said Jones, turning away from Bradford, "seems you might enter eternity soon if I don't take care of this! There's a problem with the rigging. Good day, Bradford."

Over the next few weeks, more of the passengers got sick. Some were confined to their beds. The ones who weren't sick whispered about a mutiny. "The voyage is taking too long," they said. "The crew mistreats us. Maybe Captain Jones has swindled us!"

Brewster, the minister, reminded them that God does not bless mutinies.

Bradford stood on the prow most afternoons, except when the weather forced him to remain below. It was always cold, and he burrowed into his oilskin coat and brimmed hat to keep warm. But he watched eagerly for any sign of land, and asked the crew questions about their progress. When it wasn't raining, he brought out his journal and made notes about the weather, who was sick, and how many supplies they had left. He looked forward to the day when his son would read about the journey.

"All I see is water!" declared one of the passengers, joining Bradford above decks one afternoon.

Bradford shielded his eyes with one hand. "All I see is your red hair, Standish."

Miles Standish chuckled. An army captain, he wore a rust-colored uniform with braided stripes on the sleeves and white cuffs. He was short, his head reaching only to Bradford's shoulders. But he made up for his height with his blazing red hair and his matching temper. Their friend Edward Winslow called him the "little chimney" for a reason.

"How long until we reach land?" Standish asked, gazing out at the endless water.

"Not long, I think," said Bradford.

"I hope you're right. We ran out of turnips and potatoes a week ago. All we have left are beans, smoked herring, salt pork, and the spices each passenger brought for himself."

"I know. But God will provide. He already has, just by including you in our midst. John Carver was wise to recommend you. We need your military training to help us scout a location and food source for the colony."

"I've learned some survival skills in my lifetime," Standish agreed. But he chewed on his mustache as he hesitated.

"What's the problem?"

"Consider me a friend, Bradford, but I'm not part of your separatist congregation. Many of us who are not a part of your congregation may want our own colony."

"We must stay together if we are to survive," insisted Bradford. "Our purpose isn't to force everyone to worship like us. We just want the freedom to worship according to our convictions. There is no reason we can't form a united colony."

A drop of rain landed on his nose. Both men looked up at the sky. The wind was picking up and the clouds were churning faster and darker.

"Another storm!" groaned Standish.

"They do blow in quickly this time of year. I guess we better..."

A woman's scream came from below. Bradford and Miles

looked at each other in alarm and ran for the stairs. The rain was already pelting them, soaking their shoulders before they arrived below decks.

The scream had come from one of the few private cabins. Brewster was outside the door with a young man named Stephen Hopkins.

"What's happening?" demanded Standish.

"It's Hopkin's wife," said Brewster. "She's about to give birth."

"Now?" Bradford frowned.

The wind began to howl above them. Hopkins's face was white.

"Come with me," insisted Standish, taking Hopkins by the arm. "Take it from an experienced soldier—we need to leave this job to those who know best!" He led the panic-stricken husband away.

Brewster shook his head. "This ship is no place to be giving birth."

"Especially during a storm!" said Bradford.

"A midwife is with her, and several other women. But the baby is early. She expected to have gone ashore before she had to deliver."

The ship was rocking now. Inside the tiny cabin, the woman's moans grew louder.

Dorothy Bradford appeared in the passage. She said nothing to her husband, but shoved a bundle into his arms and went into the cabin.

Bradford looked down at the bundle. It was a baby's christening gown. Dorothy had not finished the neat row of embroidery along the hem.

Concern creased Brewster's forehead. "Your wife sinks deeper into melancholy, my friend. I regret that your family had to be separated."

"As do I," Bradford said with a sigh. "But I am convinced the Lord called our people to this voyage. I trust that he will bring my family together again. Is it not a good sign that he is blessing our congregation with a new life even now?" He had to clutch at the cabin door to keep his footing.

"We may be adding one to our number," said Brewster, frowning, "but we're about to lose one as well."

"What do you mean?"

"William Butten, the servant of Dr. Fuller, is near death. I've spent many hours with him, praying that God in his providence would heal him, but I'm afraid he doesn't have long."

"The Lord gives and the Lord takes away," Bradford quoted from the Scriptures.

Brewster nodded and finished the verse: "Blessed be the name of the Lord."

A few days later, the crew wrapped the body of William Butten in sailcloth. Brewster led the funeral service on deck. Accompanied by the singing of psalms, Butten's body was placed on a plank and slid into the ocean. In the background, a newborn baby cried.

When the service was over, Bradford turned to find Stephen and Elizabeth Hopkins with their child. "Have you decided on a name yet?" he asked, touching the baby's soft cheek.

"Yes, we have." Elizabeth looked weak, but she smiled at her son and held him close to her blue dress. "We're going to call him Oceanus."

"An apt name," Bradford agreed.

Brewster made his way over to them. "May I have a word with you?" he said to Bradford.

The Hopkins excused themselves, and the two men moved to the railing.

"With so many sick, and now Butten's death, the crew and passengers are becoming more discontent," said Brewster. "Talk of mutiny continues. I have to keep reminding everyone that a mutiny will not honor God or get us any closer to our goal."

"It has been a hard journey. We're all ready to set our feet on solid ground again."

"I'm afraid we won't find much unity among the people when we do land, even among our own congregation. And the others have less reason to cooperate with us."

"Perhaps we should draw up an agreement," Bradford suggested. "We can ask the passengers to sign a statement of unity before we arrive. Each of us should commit to making our new colony successful."

Brewster nodded. "It's a good idea. It might encourage people. I will speak to Standish and Carver and ask them to draft a document."

He went below to find Carver.

The next day, Captain Jones spotted driftwood floating off the bow of the *Mayflower*. Later that day, a seagull landed near the helm. The crew began to take soundings to check the depth of the water.

Word spread quickly that the journey was almost over.

A great cheer erupted a few days later when the sailor up in the crow's nest cried, "Land Ho! Land Ho!" Captain Jones climbed up with his telescope to see for himself.

Dozens of passengers ran above decks to catch a glimpse of the shore. At first all they could see was the choppy, gray sea stretching out forever. But then, slowly, a dark line appeared at the horizon. It grew thicker as they approached.

"Virginia!" someone shouted. "That is Virginia! We made it!"

People fell to their knees on the deck. Some thanked God for delivering them from the sea. Others begged his forgiveness for considering mutiny. Tears of joy rolled down their faces.

Bradford breathed a great sigh of relief.

A few hours later, Captain Jones called for Bradford to meet him in his cabin. It was a small room, with a bed, sideboard, and a table bolted to the floor. A level row of portholes offered a view of the main deck.

Standish, Brewster, and Carver were already there with Jones.

They did not look as happy as they had earlier.

"Is there a problem?" asked Bradford.

Captain Jones pulled him over to a map spread across the table. "We're too far north," he said, poking a long fingernail at a spot on the map. "We're near Cape Cod."

Carver leaned over the table. "Our land charter is for this area down here."

"So we need to head south, toward the Hudson River," said Bradford.

Carver nodded.

"The problem is," spoke up Standish, "that the water is too rough here. The captain wants to put out to sea again and then head south. With this wind, it will take a few days."

"The passengers are not going to like that," warned Brewster, shaking his head. "They're ready to get off this boat."

Jones shrugged. "It's the only thing we can do. The winter currents have pulled us too far off course."

"Do it then," said Bradford. "I hate to lose sight of land, too, but we have no choice. Carver and I will just explain to the people."

So the crew of the *Mayflower* put out to sea again, and began to head south. But the tides were treacherous and they could make little headway. Supplies were nearly gone. After a few days, they were forced to turn north again.

This time, they passed Cape Cod. Further on they found a large bay with still water where they could safely land.

But some of the passengers were angry.

"This is not the territory granted in our charter," said Stephen Hopkins.

Most of the men were gathered around a table in the great cabin, looking over a map Carver had spread out.

"We cannot be forced to settle in an uncharted land!" insisted Hopkins. "It's too dangerous!"

Several men murmured in agreement.

"It's more dangerous to keep looking for another harbor," argued Bradford. "And it's impossible to turn back now."

"No one will force anyone to do anything," said Brewster. "But it would be foolish to go our separate ways. United we have a better chance of survival. The Holy Scriptures teach us that a house divided cannot stand."

The men were silent.

"We all want to build a better world for our children," said Bradford. "We came here to start a community in the name of God where our children are free to live, farm, and worship without fear. We can agree on that, can't we?"

They nodded.

"Good. Now, some of us have been talking about just how to do this. Carver?"

"We can each bring our God-given gifts to make this a better world for our children," said Carver. "We will govern ourselves. We will elect our leaders according to a majority vote. We will have equality under the law. That is what we are all seeking, yes?"

Heads bobbed in agreement.

Carver unfurled a sheet of paper on top of the map. "That's why we have drafted this document. It describes how we will covenant with one another to plant a new society for the glory of God. We will create just and equal laws for the good of our colony. And then we promise to obey those laws."

He picked up a quill pen and signed his name across the bottom with a flourish. "Who else will sign this covenant in the presence of God and one another?" He held out the pen.

"I will," declared Bradford. He made his mark on the page below Carver's.

"I will, too," said Brewster, reaching for the pen.

"Who else is with us?" called Bradford.

The men glanced at each other around the table.

"Count me in!" came a shout.

The crowd parted as Miles Standish moved to the center. He was one of the few men that didn't have to tilt his head to one side to stand upright under the low ceiling. The lamplight set his red hair aflame.

"Look, Brewster and Bradford are overbearing at times," he began.

Bradford wondered how this was going to help.

"I'm not a part of Brewster's congregation," Standish continued, "and I may never be. I'm a military man, not a religious man. But I agree with what is written here. I can work and live with these men. I can stand with them and build a free community. I think we all can! And further, I think John Carver should be our governor, and I am willing to call for a vote on that right now. Who's with me?"

Edward Winslow stepped forward. "I agree with Standish. Give me the pen, Carver. I'll sign it."

"So will I," said John Howland.

Winslow looked skeptical. "An indentured man? Why would a servant sign it?"

Carver nodded. "This document is all about the beginning of a free society. Howland won't be indentured to me for long." He smiled at the young man. "I know he can become a great leader if we give him the opportunity."

"Very well," said Winslow, and passed Howland the pen.

Within a few minutes, forty-one signatures had been put to the *Mayflower Compact*.

"We're agreed to find a place to settle," said Miles. "When will we begin exploration?"

"Tomorrow is the Sabbath," reminded Brewster. "Let's begin on Monday."

With the *Mayflower* anchored a mile offshore, Brewster's congregation spent their first Sunday in the New World as they always did. Four hours of preaching, prayer, and psalm singing in the morning were followed by another four hours of the same in the evening. The children sat on the floor and tried not to fidget.

On Monday morning, some of the passengers set out in the longboat to row to the beach. Bradford tried to get his wife to go with them, but she insisted she was needed on board to help care for the sick. So he climbed into the boat behind the Brewster family.

The air was brisk and the water icy, but they had waited so long to stand on solid ground again! Standish posted several sentries armed with muskets. The women began to wash clothes on the rocks. The men dug for clams. The children raced their dogs up and down the beach, shouting with delight.

A few men followed the beach a little further into the woods.

"It's frozen, but looks like good soil," said Hopkins.

"Look at all the trees—oaks, pines, junipers, maples, birches," counted Carver. "Let's take some firewood back to the ship."

Bradford laughed, startled, as a flock of geese swooped up around them into the air. "We could have fresh meat tonight!"

They rowed back to the ship to give their first account of the land.

"We need to put an exploration party together and take the shallop around the bay to look for a good spot," said Carver.

Captain Jones ordered his crewmen to inspect the shallop. The smaller, single-mast ship was stored in pieces below decks. Assembled, it would hold twenty men and enough supplies for a short trip.

"It took some damage in the storms," Jones said, "but the carpenters can put it in working order in a week."

"Excellent," said Bradford. "Standish, put a party together. I'll go with you."

"I'll stay behind to keep an eye on our people," Brewster agreed. "We'll pray you have quick success."

A few days later, the second ship, one-third the size of the

Mayflower, floated off her bow. Bradford said goodbye to Dorothy. Sixteen men set off with their muskets, hunting knives, and maps to find the best location for their new colony.

During the daytime, they split up. Half of the men explored the rivers and inlets in the shallop. The other half traveled on foot into the woods. The trees were bare and the grass was brown and brittle, but they could tell that in the summer months it would be lush and green. They saw flashes of deer and wild turkeys. They came upon the ruins of an old house and found bags of dried corn stored inside. Stuffing their pockets full, they promised to pay back the owners later. They drank eagerly from ice-covered ponds, the first fresh water they'd had in three months. They dug up some curious mounds of dirt, realizing too late that it was a burial ground! Quickly, they covered the graves and kneeled in prayer.

At the end of each day, the two groups met up again on the shore. They anchored the shallop and made camp on the beach. A screen of logs and pine boughs shielded them from the winter wind and sleet. They lit a fire to cook the fish or ducks they caught that day. Standish had them take turns standing watch over the silent camp while the others slept.

Once, they saw six natives and a dog staring at them across the beach. Bradford raised a hand in greeting, but they ran away before he could say anything.

Finally, on December 11, they came upon a place marked "Plymouth" on their maps, named by another explorer before them. Fields had been cultivated here, watered by several streams full of fish. Fruit and nut trees grew in the woods. And the harbor was deep enough for the *Mayflower* to get through.

"What do you think?" said Carver. "Will this do?"

"It is the best place we have seen," agreed Bradford. He looked up at the snow falling around them. "With so many of our company sick, we cannot afford to spend any more time looking."

Standish began to pace in front of them, pointing as he talked.

"This area over here could be the fort, with the canons set up there. It makes the harbor defensible. We'll build a large common house over there until individual cottages can be put up."

Carver nodded. "We can send out hunting and fishing parties while the rest of us start building and unloading the ship."

A smile began to spread across Bradford's face as he pictured what the village might look like by summer. "It's settled then. We shall return to the *Mayflower* and lead them here to Plymouth!"

It took a full day to sail back to the ship. As the shallop approached, Captain Jones lowered a gangplank so the explorers could cross to the *Mayflower*. "Welcome aboard," he called.

Some of the passengers waited on decks to meet them. Brewster was with them.

"Good news!" cried Bradford, stepping off the plank. "Brewster, we're going to Plymouth!"

But Brewster did not smile. He put a heavy hand on Bradford's shoulder. "I don't know how to say this, my friend."

"What is it?" asked Bradford, forgetting his excitement. "Did something happen while we were away?"

The minister's face was grave. "It's your wife."

Bradford glanced around at the crowd on deck. Carver was holding up a map and describing the land to the passengers. Dorothy was not among them.

"Where is she?"

Brewster's voice was low. "She's dead."

Bradford gripped the railing. He felt for a moment like his heart had stopped. "What happened?" he whispered.

Brewster took his arm and led him to a coil of rope where they sat together. "We found her in the water. We don't know if she jumped in or if she fell overboard." He looked at his friend with compassion. "I'm sorry."

Bradford gazed away toward the shore. A biting wind was coming off the sea.

"You should change into some dry clothes," said Brewster.

"It has been a hard winter."

"Yes, and I believe it will grow harder still before spring arrives. But we have only begun our journey to the New World. We must fix our eyes upon the author and finisher of our faith."

"I need some time alone to pray."

Brewster stood. "Take all the time you need, Bradford. I will call the congregation together to thank God for guiding you and to ask him to bless our work. You are the one that said we are pilgrims in this land. But in God's providence, we have a new home."

He left Bradford sitting on the coil of rope. A cold rain began to fall, and the passengers filed below to join the minister in prayer. Captain Jones ordered his crew to hoist anchor.

The *Mayflower*, with the wind behind her, set sail for Plymouth Harbor, where hardship and freedom to worship awaited the new residents.

The arrival of the Mayflower *at Plymouth in December 1620 changed North America and the world forever. Governor John Carver and nearly half the colonists died during the first harsh winter. William Bradford was elected the second governor and served in that position almost continuously until 1656. John Howland earned his freedom and became an assistant to the governor. William Brewster preached twice every Sunday until his death in 1643. Miles Standish protected the colony as military leader for 40 years.*

As governor, Bradford forged a peaceful alliance with the native people, the Wampanoag nation, who taught the colonists how to plant crops and fish the local waters. Bradford married a widow, Alice Carpenter Southworth, who arrived in Plymouth two years after the Mayflower. *His son, John, eventually joined him. Bradford's journal, published by the title* Of Plymouth Plantation, *is the main source for the history of the Plymouth Colony and the first document to use the word "pilgrim" in reference to America's settlers.*

Samuel Rutherford: Called Before A Higher Tribunal

OCTOBER 1660. ST. ANDREWS, SCOTLAND.

THE BEDCLOTHES WERE damp with sweat, but the man shivered and burrowed deeper into his featherbed. Rain trickled against the single windowpane in his second-floor room. He tried to concentrate on the rhythm and let it lull him to sleep. But the fever made him tremble, and he was dizzy with pain.

Out on the cobblestone street, splashing hoofbeats came to a stop nearby. Muffled voices floated up from the room below. The stairs creaked, and then a rectangle of soft candlelight fell across the bed as the bedroom door opened.

"Are you awake, Samuel?"

Samuel Rutherford slowly turned his head, his gray hair matted across the pillow. "I can't sleep. Was that someone at the door?"

The woman came in and set the candlestick on the small table next to the bed.

"It was one of your students delivering a message," she said.

He didn't open his eyes.

"James Guthrie has been arrested. They are burning your books and his at the Cross of Edinburgh."

"Then it is only a matter of time before they arrest me, too," he said. He pressed his fingers against his throbbing head and slowly opened his eyes.

Tears were shining in hers.

He held his arm out to her and she sat next to him on the cot.

"Maybe it's not too late," she said. "Maybe we can convince them that you are not worth this trouble."

"I have written what I have written, Jean. No amount of pleading from me or my wife will change the opinions of King Charles or Parliament."

"But Charles said he would support the National Covenant!"

"The first act of his restoration as king was to break his covenant. All kings consider themselves above the law. Henry, James, the first Charles, and now his son—their right to rule is the one thing they will not allow us to question. But it is our responsibility as loyal subjects to remind them of their duty to the law of God."

She picked at the loose stitching at her apron hem. "Your letters are always persuasive. Maybe you can write a letter."

"And take back everything I preached for thirty-five years? No. They will accuse me of treason, but I will not be subject to a tyrant, be he pope or king. Besides, I once preached a sermon in Charles's presence about his duty. His opinion of me was settled then."

"What about your family?"

He took her hand. "The hardship on you and the girls is my one regret. But you know I would rather die than stop fighting for what is biblical and right for Scotland."

She was quiet. For a few moments, the only sound was the patter of rain against the window. But then a child's weak cough came from the next room.

"I have to check on Margaret," said Jean, standing. "She has grown as sick as you."

"Kiss her for me."

She took the candle and went out, shutting the door with a soft click.

He was shaking again, and tried to wrap the blanket tighter around his chest. Guthrie's arrest was not a surprise. Guthrie was one of the most vocal of the Covenanters. He had not taken credit for the pamphlet *The Causes of the Lord's Wrath*, but everyone knew he had written it. Like Rutherford's own book, *Lex Rex*, it argued that the Bible had some pretty strong things to say about the way a king ruled his people. But then, so did the National Covenant.

"Guthrie," Rutherford thought in his bed, "you were right. When we signed it, you said the National Covenant would someday lead to your death."

The fever made bright spots of color dance behind his closed eyes. But his memory was vivid of the scene in Edinburgh more than twenty years ago.

It was February. Frost covered the small white headstones dotting the Greyfriars Churchyard. In the brisk air, the stained glass windows of the church glittered like colored ice. Dozens of ministers had lined up in the yard, one by one stepping up to a large sheet of paper unrolled on a table. Rutherford stamped his feet to keep warm and scanned the churchyard for Guthrie. His friend was quite short and hard to spot in a crowd.

"Samuel!"

He turned. "There you are."

Guthrie's thick eyebrows were raised in amusement. "You won't believe who I bumped into on my way here! I mean, I almost knocked the man over."

"Who?" Rutherford steered them into line.

"The city executioner!" Guthrie exclaimed. "It was as if God was telling me I was on my way to sign my own death sentence."

Rutherford chuckled. "Nonsense. This National Covenant honors God. We are calling the nation to recommit to Reformation theology and Presbyterianism, and to oppose all human innovations in worship. God will bless this, James."

"This will lead to war," insisted Guthrie. "But a war to secure the Reformation in Scotland is worth my life."

"If John Knox was alive today, he'd put his signature on this covenant."

"It does reaffirm the confession of faith he gave to Scotland."

"And we have public support," said Rutherford. "Riots broke out everywhere when the king tried to impose the English prayer book. An organized resistance by the leaders of Scotland is a far better solution than public mayhem." He stepped up to the page and took the pen offered him. "There!" he said with satisfaction, scrawling his name. "Your turn, James."

Guthrie took the pen and leaned over the table. "I'm telling you, this is my death warrant. But I'm certain it is the right thing to do."

In his bed, an older Rutherford remembered his friend's words. Thousands across Scotland had eagerly signed the National Covenant. Rutherford became a leading member of the Covenanter clergy, and took a post as minister in St. Andrews and professor at the university. He took part in local elections, organized prayer meetings and fasts, and wrote hundreds of letters.

But that was during the reign of the first King Charles. After Charles was beheaded by the English Parliament, the new Lord Protector Cromwell invaded Scotland. Thousands of Covenanters were killed in uprisings and battles. The king's son promised he would uphold the Covenant if Scotland helped him regain his father's throne. But as soon as he was crowned, he went back on his word and started arresting the Covenanters.

"Guthrie was right," Rutherford thought. "Our leadership in the Covenant might now lead to our deaths. But he would sign it again today. And so would I."

With his friend's peril on his mind, the fever finally carried him into a troubled sleep.

In the next room, a slim girl in a simple, rust-colored dress was bathing the face of a younger girl tucked into bed. "It's all right, Margaret," she murmured. "When you wake up in the morning, I will come sing to you again."

Jean came in carrying a pewter cup. "She is still awake?"

The young woman nodded. "Her fever is worse," she said.

"I brought her some water," her mother said. "Let me take over for awhile, Agnes. Will you go downstairs and mind the stew?"

Agnes squeezed her sister's hand and slipped out the door.

Jean held the cup to the girl's lips. "Another sip, Margaret."

She drank obediently, dribbling water on the blanket.

Jean set the cup on the floor. "Better?"

Margaret gave a little nod. "Agnes says Father is in trouble." Her voice was raspy.

"It is nothing you should worry about," assured her mother.

"He is sick like me."

"Yes, he is. You two are very much alike, aren't you?" She kissed the girl's cheek. "Try to get some more rest, all right? I'll bring you more water later."

The girl snuggled further under the quilt and closed her eyes.

A few evenings later there was another knock on the front door. Jean Rutherford plucked her bonnet from her pocket and put it on, letting the ribbons dangle, and went to the door.

The man on the stoop was dressed all in black. Water streamed off the brim of his hat and onto his shoulders.

"Mr. Blair," she said, stepping aside so he could enter. "We weren't expecting you today."

He knocked his hat against the door frame to shake off the water. "I'm sorry for calling so late, Mrs. Rutherford," he said. "But I need to speak with Samuel immediately."

She led him up the stairs, but her husband was not in his bed.

"He is not well," she said. "He would have risen only to see Margaret."

They peeked into the second room. Samuel sat on the floor next to his daughter's narrow cot. She lay on her back, clutching one of his hands in her two small ones. Her face was white, except for spots of feverish pink high on her cheeks. Her eyes were squinted tightly shut in prayer.

"There are so many enemies in this life, Lord," Rutherford was praying aloud, "and Satan is never so happy as when thy servants are sick and incapable of being about thy business."

Jean and Blair stood quietly in the doorway and listened.

"When we decay, Lord, we look for thy mercy," Rutherford prayed. "Humble us and heal us. In thy grace, we ask to be steadfast. We bring our burdens to thee, knowing thou will care for us. Grant us the hope we can find only in the Lord Christ. Amen."

Margaret kissed her father's hand. "Amen," she whispered.

"Now will you sleep?" he said gently, brushing the damp hair from her forehead.

"I will try to sleep if you will," she said with a little smile.

"It's a covenant then." He struggled to his feet.

In two steps, Mr. Blair reached him and caught his arm. "Perhaps you shouldn't make covenants so eagerly," said Blair. "They seem to be a continuing source of trouble for you."

"It is far too late to change that," Rutherford muttered.

Blair helped him back to his room, with Jean following. "Margaret does not appear to be better," the visitor said to her.

"She grows worse," she said sadly.

"How old is she now? Four?"

"Five."

He looked at the Rutherfords with compassion. "I am sorry to bring you more bad news. But there is something you should see." He went to the window and drew aside the shutter. "Look toward the university."

Samuel leaned on his wife's arm and moved to the window. The glass was streaked with rain, but beyond the blurry jumble of doorsteps and chimneys, the university buildings were illuminated by an orange glow.

Rutherford turned back to his bed. "They are burning my books," he said.

Blair nodded. "And the Committee of Estates declared today that they will issue a summons for your appearance. Expect it to arrive tomorrow or the following day."

Rutherford fell back on his pillow, exhausted, and pulled the quilt up to his chin. "I can barely get out of bed. How can I appear for trial?"

"You'll be charged with treason for writing that book."

"I never meant to say anything disloyal or treasonous against the king personally. God is my witness! But I have spoken and written according to my conscience, as informed by God's Word. It is my duty as a minister to say these things."

"Aye, but they will hang you on the scaffold for it!" declared Blair. Immediately, he wished he hadn't said that in front of Mrs. Rutherford. He glanced at her, ashamed, but she met his eyes with resolve.

"I will face the scaffold for that book with a good conscience," Rutherford insisted. "That is, if they can drag this weak body up there." His eyes were closed, and he smiled with a memory. "You and I were at the Westminster Assembly when I published that book, Robert. Remember?"

"You published quite a few books during those years. I don't know when you found the time to write with all those meetings."

It seemed like only yesterday to Rutherford, though it was really seventeen years ago. Parliament had called the ministers together at Westminster Abbey in London to discuss matters of theology and church government. Rutherford was one of eight commissioners sent to represent the Scottish church.

Every morning, the full assembly met to debate. Every afternoon, they split into three committees and drafted documents for discussion. It took them nearly four years, but they finally produced an impressive document known as the *Westminster Confession of Faith*.

And Rutherford had produced a few documents of his own. By the time he left London to return to St. Andrews, he had published several books—including the one that was now getting him in trouble.

"When the first King Charles read my book," said Rutherford, "he said it would 'scarcely get an answer.'"

"I think a bonfire worth of copies is an answer," said Blair.

Rutherford's face was sober. "Is there news of Guthrie?"

Blair glanced away. "He has been transferred to the tower of Stirling. It does not look good for him."

"He didn't get the nickname 'Sure Foot' for nothing," said Rutherford. "He'll stand his ground."

"Poor James," Jean murmured. "How is his family?"

"They are struggling," admitted Blair, "especially his wife. But the congregation is taking good care of them."

"Oh, that is another knock on the door," said Jean, moving to the window. "They haven't come to arrest Samuel, have they?"

Blair shook his head. "No, the Committee of Estates doesn't move that fast. It will be Dr. Burnett. He said he would meet me here."

"Soon we'll have the whole congregation of St. Andrews at my bedside!" said Rutherford.

Jean propped her husband up with another pillow, and went downstairs to get the door. A moment later the doctor appeared in the bedroom doorway.

Rutherford raised his head. "Come in, Doctor. We were just discussing the impending glory of heaven."

"Death is not something to treat lightly," Burnett scolded, ducking through the doorway. He had left his coat and hat downstairs, but carried his satchel of instruments with him. It was wet with rain, and he set it on the floor and wiped his hand on his knee breeches.

"Neither is it something to fear," said Rutherford.

"I have heard you preach that many a time," replied the doctor. "But as you are in bed and I am still on my feet, you will let me do the preaching today, agreed?" He leaned over his patient. "Now let me listen to you breathe."

Rutherford drew in a deep, ragged breath. "It's Margaret you should be checking on," he wheezed.

"I will see her before I go," Burnett promised. "You are still eating?"

"The broth Jean brings me every day. But I barely have the strength to use the chamber pot, and the fever brings on wild nightmares."

"I will send you another bottle of tonic. But I doubt it will help you much now, Samuel." He stood up and jerked a thumb toward Blair. "I ran into Mr. Blair in front of the university an hour ago. The bonfire was hard to miss, though it was sputtering in the rain. He told me the Estates is summoning you."

"The doctor is going to submit a plea to stall a trial in light of your health," said Blair.

Burnett shrugged. "Perhaps a letter from me and a letter from the university rector will convince them," he said. "You're in no condition to offer a sound defense at trial."

Agnes walked by the open door on her way to Margaret's room, and the men could hear her singing quietly to her sister.

Rutherford passed a hand over his eyes and looked up at the doctor. "I am willing to die for the cause of Christ and Scotland, but I am grateful for every day with my family. I will not object to a delay in trial."

"Good," said Burnett. "I will send a letter immediately, and let you know the moment I hear from them."

"Thank you. Now, gentlemen," he said, turning his face away

from them. "I am weary with talking. If you will excuse me, I have a covenant to keep with my daughter."

"And I must check in on her," Burnett said, picking up his bag. "Good night, Samuel."

The doctor slipped into the next room, and Blair went downstairs to collect his hat.

Rutherford tried to shut out the pain and go to sleep. But the memories of his past kept flashing back in his wakefulness and in his dreams. He began to think God was preparing him for the end.

A few weeks passed. When Blair arrived, the news was good and bad. The Estates had postponed Rutherford's trial due to his sickness. But in the meantime, he was under house arrest.

"House arrest?" said Rutherford, coughing. "I can't get down the stairs to the first floor. How could I ever flee the city?"

"That's not the bad news," said Blair. "They have also stripped you of your position at the university. You no longer have a job or a pension."

"How will we buy food and medicine?" cried Jean.

"The congregation will care for you," Blair promised. "We will see you have whatever you need."

"Thank you, Robert," said Rutherford.

"It is our Christian duty," Blair replied. "And it is the least we can do for the family that has served us for so many years."

He was true to his word, and came nearly every day to bring them supplies and encouragement.

Winter arrived in St. Andrews. A few large snowflakes were circling outside the window when Rutherford opened his eyes one morning. Jean had brought him extra blankets, but he still shivered in his bed. He heard Margaret's weak cough in the next room.

Agnes came in with a steaming bowl of broth. "Good morning, Father. Will you eat?"

"For you, my dear, I will try." He gave her a feeble smile. "Push that table a little closer."

She helped him sit up in bed and sip from the bowl.

"What day is it?"

"15 February."

"Then Guthrie's trial is set to begin in five days," he said. "I must write to him. Bring me my pen and some paper."

She came back with the supplies and cleared his bowl from the table. "Do you want me to write it for you?"

"Thank you, no," he said. "Your mother needs your help. I think I can still hold my pen."

He could still hold the pen, but leaning over the table proved to be an effort. He pulled the blankets tighter around his shoulders and hunched over the paper and wrote:

Dear Brother,

Forget not the promises and providence of God. Our lives are as brief and frail as a green herb. Do not think it strange that men devise against you. But remember this. If you face exile, the earth is the Lord's. If you face continued imprisonment, the Lord is your liberty. If you face a violent death, the kingdom of heaven consists of a fair company of martyrs. Do not fear, and forgive your enemies. For it is certain that Jesus Christ, prince of the kings of the earth, will reign. The Lord's salvation will not tarry! And your blood is precious in his sight. Now, cast your wife and children on the Lord Christ. He cares for you and them.

Your own brother, S.R.

He was startled by Jean's urgent cry from the other room. "Samuel! Samuel, get up!"

Shoving the table aside, he swung his stiff legs over the bed. "Jean? What is it?"

"Hurry!"

Head spinning, he stumbled through the door and into the next room. Agnes stood in the corner, one hand to her mouth. His wife was bent over Margaret, raising her up by her shoulders. But the little girl's body was limp.

"She is burning up with fever. I can't wake her!"

He collapsed on his knees beside the bed and took his daughter's hands in his. "Margaret, my love. Can you hear me? Margaret?"

Jean whirled toward the older girl. "Agnes, you must run for Dr. Burnett. Hurry!"

Agnes shot a tearful glance at her unconscious sister and then flew down the stairs. The door slammed in the room below, rattling the upstairs window.

Margaret's breathing was so shallow, her father could not hear her draw breath. Only the slight rise and fall of the blanket over her chest told him she was still breathing.

His head throbbed. He shut his eyes and tried to focus his thoughts on words of prayer. But his eyes flew open again when a sob burst from his wife.

Margaret's covers had stopped moving. She lay still and silent, her golden hair spread across the pillow.

Hot tears streamed down his face. He leaned over the girl and kissed her damp forehead. "I'll see you soon, my daughter," he whispered.

Whether by execution or sickness, he knew it was only a matter of time.

He drew his wife into his arms and held her until the doctor came. He didn't have the strength to stand up. Burnett had to carry him back to his bed.

He was too ill to go to the churchyard for Margaret's burial.

A month later, on the streets of St. Andrews, Robert Blair knocked on the Rutherford's door. Dr. Burnett and a few members of the congregation were with him.

"They wanted to say good bye," he explained to Jean, removing his hat. "Is it all right?"

"Of course," she said. Methodically, she untied her apron and hung it on a hook by the door. "Agnes is reading to him in his room. Follow me."

Her shoes clicked on the stairs. They fell into step behind her, climbing as quietly as possible. At the top, they crowded into the tiny room.

The light outside the window was already fading. Agnes had lit an oil lamp on the table, casting a gentle circle of yellow light just around the bed. The girl was sitting in a straight-backed chair with a New Testament on her lap. Rutherford was listening, eyes closed. He was propped up against the pillows, a black shawl tucked around his thin shoulders.

"It's Mr. Blair and Dr. Burnett, Father," she said, looking up from the Bible.

Rutherford slowly turned to his visitors. His face appeared gray.

"I apologize for the interruption," said Blair. "But I have news, and these dear friends wanted to come along and see you."

Rutherford coughed, and when he spoke, his voice was hoarse. "You are all welcome."

"What is the news?" asked Jean.

Robert handed her a sheet of paper from inside his coat. "Parliament has reviewed the Estates' accusation against Samuel." He looked at the dying man. "They are calling you to stand trial in Edinburgh on charges of treason."

"I'm afraid they won't get to hang me," Rutherford replied. "I'm near to eternity now. I'm being called before a higher tribunal than Parliament!"

"And in this case," said Burnett, "the judge is your friend."

Rutherford smiled. "Aye, and he never breaks his covenant! I have spent my life defending the crown rights of the Redeemer. It is no easy thing to be a Christian, but at the end, the king of heaven embraces us."

Agnes put a hand on her father's arm.

He looked at her tenderly. "Do not worry, dear ones," he said. "I am leaving you all in the secure care of our Lord. I go not to death, but to glory. Glory shines in Emmanuel's kingdom! And by tomorrow, I shall be there, adoring him."

The floorboards squeaked as the visitors shifted to let Jean move toward the bed. She took her husband's hand.

Blair gathered them in a half circle around the family. "Let us share a taste of that glory," he said. He began to sing a psalm in his rich, steady tenor, and they all joined in.

When the song was finished, Rutherford had a word of encouragement for each person. Each one filed past his bed, then slipped soberly down the stairs and out into the crisp evening air.

By morning, he was gone. But when Jean kissed him good bye, his face was peaceful and smiling. He had stepped, rejoicing, into the kingdom of his covenant-keeping God.

Rutherford was rescued from the gallows by his natural death on March 29, 1661. But James Guthrie and many other Covenanters were hanged for their opposition to King Charles's interference in how they could worship God. Guthrie was reported to have shouted, "The Covenants, the Covenants, will yet be revived in Scotland!" as he died. For years, there would be many battles and uprisings. The National Covenant was never made official again, though its principles were implemented later in 1690 with the Act of Settlement.

Rutherford's work helped establish in Scotland what is known as the Presbyterian form of church government. Of all of his writings, his letters became the most popular because of their devotional qualities. More than eighty editions of his collected letters have been published in English.

CONFESSIONS AND CATECHISMS OF THE REFORMATION

WHEN THE ANCIENT and medieval Christians met in councils, it was to decide important church business. This often meant discussing the teachings of Scripture and making it official church doctrine by drafting a *creed*, or a short statement of beliefs. During the Reformation, as so many doctrines were being debated, it became common to draft larger statements known as *confessions*.

The reformers believed that doctrine should only come from the Bible. They argued that sometimes the pope and church councils had made decisions about doctrine on their own authority and not always on the authority of Scripture. So to correct that error, the reformers decided to draft confessions based only on the teaching of Scripture. Many of these confessions were also useful for identifying which beliefs Protestants had in common with each other. This became a way of uniting them in the essential teachings of the Bible, and led to the slogan "In essentials unity, in non-essentials liberty, in all things charity."

Anabaptists wrote the first confession of the Reformation in 1527 called the *Schleitheim Confession*. This document rejected teachings by the Lutheran reformers as well as the teachings of Rome. German Lutherans wrote the *Augsburg Confession* (1530) as part of the Peace of Augsburg. In Geneva, Calvin and Farel wrote the *Geneva Confession* (1536) as a statement of Christian doctrine for the people of the city. And in Zürich, the *First Helvetic Confession* (1536) was composed by Heinrich Bullinger and Ulrich Zwingli for the German residents of Switzerland.

Other confessions soon took the stage, including the *French Confession* (1559), John Knox's *Scots Confession* (1560), the *Belgic Confession* (1561), and the *Second Helvetic Confession* (1566).

To teach the confessions, the reformers used *catechisms*, a word meaning "to instruct." These catechisms are summaries of doctrine in the form of questions with answers. For example, the first question of the *Westminster Shorter Catechism* (1647) is "What is the chief end of man?" The answer is "Man's chief end is to glorify God and enjoy him forever." The question and answer format helped people avoid false teachings by better understanding and remembering the Bible. Early catechisms included Luther's *Larger and Smaller Catechisms* (1529), the *Geneva Catechism* (1541), and the *Heidelberg Catechism* (1562).

Under Queen Elizabeth I, the *Thirty-Nine Articles* (1563) became the official statement of the Church of England. But not all Christians in England were satisfied with this document. The *Puritans* believed the Articles contained statements of error.

The Puritans were a later generation of reformers who sought greater reforms in the Church of England. They often identified themselves with John Calvin. They believed the Church of England had mixed in too much Catholic teaching with the Protestant teaching. Because they refused to conform and separated themselves from the official church, they were called *non-conformists* or *separatists*. Some of the most famous Puritans were

William Ames, John Bunyan, John Owen, Samuel Rutherford, and Richard Baxter.

The Puritans also objected to the *Book of Common Prayer*. This is not a confession or catechism, but a collection of prayers and readings for worship. The Puritans said the ceremonies in the book were too much like Catholic ceremonies. When King Charles I of England came to the throne, he and William Laud, the Archbishop of Canterbury, tried to impose the book on Scotland. Scottish Puritans refused, leading to military conflicts between Scotland and England. The English Parliament—with a strong Puritan faction—signed a treaty called *The Solemn League and Covenant* with the Scots to overthrow Charles.

As part of that agreement, Parliament set out to correct what the Puritans believed was wrong with the Church of England. That process began in 1643 with the *Westminster Assembly*. Ministers from England and Scotland met at Westminster Abbey in London to revise the *Thirty-Nine Articles*. But they eventually abandoned that goal and by 1647 had instead produced the *Westminster Confession of Faith*. To this day, it is the most influential of all Reformed confessions in the English-speaking world.

Other Protestants continued to write confessions, including a modification of the *Westminster Confession* by Baptists, published as the *1689 London Baptist Confession*.

Today, confessions are still used by millions of Christians across the globe as a way of communicating and uniting over their beliefs.

J⊕HN BUNYAN: WHEN I FALL, I ARISE

JUNE 1677. BEDFORD GAOL, BEDFORDSHIRE, ENGLAND.

THE ONLY WINDOW in the cell was crosshatched with iron bars. But the prisoner didn't mind. He thought it cast interesting shadows, little crosses repeating across the wooden door and the weathered stone walls on the opposite side.

He was seated at a low table next to a cot. A tall stack of papers and a neat row of ink pots covered the tabletop. His back ached from sitting on a wicker stool that offered no support, but he was absorbed in his thoughts and barely noticed.

Absent-mindedly, he fished an ivory comb out of his pocket and parted his mustache. His strong jaw and piercing eyes gave him an aristocratic air. But the broad cuffs at the end of his sleeves were shiny with wear, and a few buttons were missing from the front of his shirt. He slipped the comb back into his pocket and started to read aloud the text in front of him. The echo of his voice was the only sound in the chamber. As his imagination took over, he felt the cell walls fade away to a dark hillside in the other world of the book.

He was looking through the eyes of a young man named Christian, on a long, dangerous journey.

Christian carried a sword and a knapsack. He was following a twisting path that led down into a dark, rocky field. An ancient signpost on the roadside said "Valley of Humiliation."

That didn't sound very encouraging.

Stepping cautiously into the barren field, he noticed movement out of the corner of his eye. Turning, he gasped to see a frightful monster coming toward him! The creature was covered in fish scales, had the bony wings of a dragon, moved on the huge paws of a bear, and snarled with a lion's jaw. His belly glowed with fire.

"I am Apollyon the Destroyer!" roared the creature.

Christian wanted to run, but he had no armor on his back. He knew that if he turned away, the monster would attack him from behind. So he raised his two-edged sword, faced the beast, and planted his feet firmly in the valley soil.

"Where did you come from?" demanded Apollyon. "And where are you going?"

Christian swallowed hard. "I am from the city of Destruction, the place of all evil, but I am going to the city of Zion."

"I am the prince and god of the city of Destruction," cried Apollyon. "So you are one of my subjects. Why are you running from your king?"

Christian began to back away. The beast was still half a field away, but he was far too close for comfort. "I was born in your domain, but your service was hard and your wages poor," he stammered. "The wages of sin is death. I am seeking liberation from that sin."

Apollyon roared, smoke pouring from his belly. "No prince will let his subject go so easily," he growled. He twisted his head left and right, peering down at the little man with his fiery eyes. "Go back to your country and serve me, or I will strike you down."

"I have given myself to the king of princes," said Christian. "I cannot in fairness go back with you."

Apollyon stomped his huge bear paws. The earth quaked with a thunderous rumble. "Then you have left the bad for the worse. See if the prince will let you go and return to me."

Christian flinched, but he would not back down. "The prince I have sworn to follow now will forgive the sins I committed when I followed you. His kingdom is far better than yours."

Orange flames leaped from Apollyon's stomach. "I kill his servants. But my servants live with power and all the riches of the world."

"The death you give his servants is nothing but glory for us. It is deliverance from this world."

Apollyon howled with rage and sprang forward. His size seemed to double with every leap, leaving steaming craters in his footsteps.

But Christian did not budge.

"I swear by my infernal den," roared Apollyon, towering over him, "that you shall go no further. Here I will spill your blood!" He reached into his chest and threw out a fiery dart.

Christian deflected it with his shield and fled.

More darts followed, thick as a hailstorm. Christian could not ward off them all. One hot point pierced his shoulder, another his foot. He realized he had only one option—turn and fight. But as he swung around with his sword, the beast leaped toward him and knocked him to the ground. The sword tumbled from his hand.

Apollyon crouched over him, so close that he could feel the heat of the furnace against his legs. "You are finished," the beast grinned with blackened teeth. He drew back to make his final blow.

Quick as lightning, Christian rolled over, his fingers closing around the hilt of his sword.

"Don't rejoice over my defeat," he shouted. "When I fall, I arise!" He plunged his sword into the demon's chest.

Apollyon shrieked with pain and stumbled backwards.

"We are more than conquerors through him who loved us!" cried Christian, jumping to his feet. He charged the beast again.

But Apollyon stretched wide his leathery wings and disappeared, leaving only a trail of smoke and the echo of his roar in the hills.

The fierce battle had just concluded when a sharp knock startled the man at the table out of his imagination. The jangle of keys at his cell door brought him back to the reality of his imprisonment. He shook his head to clear it and stood up.

"I am dressed," he called out. "You may enter."

The door clanged open and the jailer looked in. "Mr. Bunyan, you have a visitor," he said.

"Thank you."

A colorful figure stepped into the cell. He was an older man, wearing a plumed hat at an angle above his long gray curls. A bit of linen trimmed the collar of his peacock green doublet, cinched at his waist with a silver buckle. He was unbuttoning his leather riding gloves as he entered.

"Mr. John Owen," said the prisoner, reaching out to shake his hand. "How good of you to come."

"Your jailer should just put your name on the door," said the visitor with a grin. "John Bunyan, tinker and bull-headed preacher, permanent resident of Bedford Gaol."

Bunyan shrugged. "At least you always know where to find me."

"One of these days I would like to talk to you over a nice dinner without the presence of armed guards."

"One of these days I would like to preach without ending up in prison!"

Owen laughed. "I am glad to see you have a more positive outlook these days."

Bunyan pulled the stool out from the desk. "I can't offer you much in the way of hospitality, but you are welcome to this very uncomfortable seat."

Owen took it, leaning back and propping up his feet on the desk. Even in the dim light of the cell, his highly polished boots shone.

Bunyan raised an eyebrow. "New boots, my friend?"

"You like them? Straight from Spain. Every man needs a good pair of boots, I say."

Bunyan settled himself on the edge of his cot. "You didn't come all the way from London to show me your boots."

"No, I came to see how you were holding up under the strain. You've been here for six months this time. Is there no hope of release?"

"The magistrate will let me go if I promise to stop preaching without a license. But what right has the Church of England to determine who can and cannot preach?"

"They fear unauthorized preaching will lead to a revolution."

"And it may. How many non-conformist preachers can they lock up? But I don't preach to stir revolution. I preach because it is in my bones. I am called to do it."

Owen nodded. "I have made the unpopular decisions as well. When I was a chaplain to Lord Protector Cromwell and the people wanted to make him king, I had to stand up and oppose them. I lost a friendship and even had to resign from my position as Vice-Chancellor of Oxford University. Secretly, I have been a minister of Presbyterian and Congregationalist churches. I have written books arguing that we must tolerate our religious differences instead of toss each other in prison."

"All actions that might have landed you in prison like me," said Bunyan. "And yet you somehow stay out of jail. You have the benefit of friends in high places."

"And therefore, so you do, my friend," said Owen. "I'm going to see what I can do for you. The Reformed church needs her defenders outside of prison. And so does your family. How are they?"

"Not well. We have never had much money, and it is harder now for Elizabeth to feed the boys."

"I was sorry to hear of your daughter's passing," said Owen. "Mary was such a kind and godly young lady."

"She reminded me of her mother," said Bunyan. "Elizabeth has been a good mother to her, but in many ways, I relied on Mary's face to remember my first wife." He frowned. "I was in prison for most of Mary's childhood."

"All the more reason to work for your release. You don't want the same thing to happen to Thomas and Joseph. I will talk to my contacts and see what I can arrange." He swung his feet from the desk and leaned over the stack of papers. "What is this? Another book?"

Bunyan nodded. "It is the one benefit of prison. If I was free, I would be busy preaching. But here, all I can do is think and write."

"What is this one about?"

"I started it the last time I was in prison and now I think it is finished. It's a bit different from my others. This one is a story about a man on a pilgrimage."

Owen picked up a few pages and scanned them. "A pilgrim named Christian. A battle with Apollyon, prince of destruction. Is this an allegory of the Christian life?"

"Yes," said Bunyan. "You see, I wanted to distract myself from the depressing thoughts of prison. And I wanted to encourage other Christians by what I have learned from my hardships. So I thought I might write a story about the struggles a Christian faces on his journey to glory. Before I knew it, all sorts of characters had come from my pen."

"You are using poetry to preach the gospel?"

"Yes, as the Bible itself often does. It helps us to understand Scripture when we can think of it as a story. Here we have Apollyon offering Christian the worthless and sinful things of this world, but Christian seeks the greatest prize, to reach the celestial city on Mount Zion. It is the story of all who strive for heaven."

"I would like to read this."

Bunyan sighed. "When I was writing it, I used to read passages to Mary when she visited me. She loved to hear about the new adventures Christian had experienced since her last visit." He held the pages out to Owen. "Here, I have already made a copy to send to my publisher someday. Please, take it with you and give me your thoughts."

"I consider it an honor," said Owen, tucking the stack under his arm. "I will return this soon, and I hope to bring good news about your release as well."

"Thank you, my friend. Would you be willing to take these letters for me, too?"

"Of course." He tucked both letters inside his doublet and picked up his gloves from the table. When he rapped at the door, the jailer appeared. "Fare thee well until I return, Mr. Bunyan."

The prisoner went back to his cot and stretched out. The shadowy crosses cast by the window bars had shifted with the sun outside. Rolling toward the wall, he stared at the small slip of paper tacked between the stones. It was a sketch of his daughter's face. He had drawn it during one of her visits, when the sun was just at the right position above the window to highlight her features.

Her face was thin. She wore her brown hair tucked simply behind her ears. But there was a gentleness in her eyes and a sweetness about her mouth that made her beautiful to him.

His first imprisonment had lasted nearly eleven years. Sometimes his compassionate jailer would let him out for a day to spend time with his family. But during the long stretches of confinement, Mary came to visit him at the jail once a week. She would bring letters, books, and fresh vegetables for the jailer to add to his dinner.

Oh, how he looked forward to those times with her! As soon as he heard her voice outside, he set down his pen and combed his mustache. He knew it was silly, because she had been blind from birth and could not tell if his whiskers were out of order. But it made him happy to prepare for her visit.

She always thanked the jailer brightly for opening the door. And then, with her walking stick in one hand, she felt her way into the cell and her father's embrace. "Hello, Father!" she would say with a smile.

"My beautiful daughter," he would reply, leading her to the seat at his desk under the barred window. "What did you bring me today?"

She would slowly pull each item out of her bundle and tell him what it was and who had sent it. Then they would talk about what was growing in the garden, who in the county had fallen ill, and where the king was traveling.

When they had caught up with the news, she would ask, "Where is Christian now?"

He would smile, pick up the latest pages on his desk, and read her a new chapter.

The first time he told her about Christian's story, they were talking about why her father was in prison.

"I have questioned the Church of England," he explained. "People like me make the king nervous. He wants me to stop preaching, so he's put me in here until I agree."

She drew her eyebrows together. "But you must obey God."

He smiled at her. "My blind daughter sees the truth better than the King of England."

"It is not easy to be a Christian."

"No, it's not," he agreed with a heavy sigh. "Sometimes we have to face Satan and stand our ground."

"Have you seen Satan?" she asked.

"I have seen him in many forms, indeed. He is the god of this world, and he seeks to destroy the followers of Christ. But the Lord Jesus is more powerful, and he aids us on our path to the heavenly Zion."

"You make it sound like an adventure."

"It *is* an adventure. In fact, I just started writing a story about the journey to Zion. The main character is a pilgrim named Christian."

Her unseeing eyes widened with excitement. "A new story! What happens?"

"Well, I haven't finished writing it yet. So I don't know how it ends. But I can tell you how it begins."

She folded her hands in her lap and turned to him with expectation.

He shuffled the stack of papers on his desk and settled onto the cot. "There was a man named Christian. One day he read a book that told him his city would soon be destroyed. He was so sad and frightened! When he returned to his house, he told his wife and children that they would all perish unless they found a way to escape."

"What did they do?"

"They thought he was losing his mind! Remember how Noah's neighbors mocked him for building the ark? The city had never been threatened before, and they had not read the warning for themselves. They didn't want to leave their home. So they refused to believe him."

"Even though destruction was coming?" She plucked at her dress with worried hands.

"Yes. Sometimes we love our current comforts so much we are willing to ignore the terrible things to come." He paused, and glanced around at the lack of comforts in his cell. "Anyway, Christian spent the night in tears, fearful that he and his family would be destroyed. But soon, he met another character, called Evangelist, who asked him why he was so disturbed. Christian told Evangelist that his city was about to be destroyed and that he was not ready to face the judgment. He was afraid he might end up in Hell if he died."

"Surely a person named Evangelist had an answer for him."

"He did. Evangelist handed the man a scroll with the words 'flee from the wrath to come' written on it. Christian begged him to tell him where he could flee to. So Evangelist pointed across a field and said, 'Do you see that gate?' But Christian couldn't see the gate. It was too far away. So Evangelist said, 'Then do you see the bright shining light?'"

"Could he see it?" asked Mary.

"He could," said Bunyan. "Evangelist told him to keep an eye on the light and he would find the gate. Once he reached the gate, he would be directed to the Mountain of Zion, the place of the celestial city."

"The celestial city," repeated Mary, rolling the name on her tongue. "Did he make it there?"

"He hasn't arrived yet," her father said, putting down the stack of paper beside him on the mattress. "But he will. First, though, he'll have to go through all sorts of trials—battles and prisons and people trying to distract him from his goal. But if he is faithful to the truth, God will bless him in the end."

"Like you," she said, reaching gently for his arm.

"I pray I will be faithful," he said, taking her hand. "I pray that for you as well."

She squeezed his hand and then touched his face, drawing her lips to his forehead in a kiss. "I love you, Father."

"And I love you, Mary."

"Perhaps I can bring you some cheese when I come next week, and you can tell me more about Christian."

"Then I'll have to keep writing!" he agreed. "Take care to arrive home safely."

"I will. Good bye." She took her walking stick and let the jailer help her back to the street.

Every visit after that, Mary asked him about the pilgrim's progress on the journey to Zion.

He read how Christian lost a great burden at a cross on a hill. "Like the cross of Jesus removes the burden of our sins," Mary said.

He described how Christian was captured by Giant Despair and locked in a cell in Doubting Castle. "Like you locked in this prison away from your family!" Mary exclaimed.

"But Christian had a key called Promise, so he could unlock any door in Doubting Castle and escape. I, too, have a key," Bunyan told Mary. "It is the Spirit of God, moving hearts to do what is right."

He told her how Christian was encouraged on his journey by fellow pilgrims named Faithful and Hopeful. Hopeful tells Christian, "Brother, I see the gate, and I see the saints standing by to receive us." Mary's face shone as she said, "Like Mother, who waits eagerly for us in Heaven!"

"Yes, just like that," he said softly.

And now, Mary, too, was waiting eagerly for him in Heaven. He gazed at the drawing of her on the wall as he lay in his cot. He wanted to tell her that he had finished the story. Christian had waded through a deep river and come at last to the celestial city, where he was given harps and crowns, and all the bells of the city rang in celebration of his arrival.

"But I don't need to tell Mary how it ends," he reminded himself. "She has finished the journey. She has arrived at the celestial city before me. She could finish this story better than I!" He missed her, and he missed his wife and his sons, who still waited for his release.

He rose from the cot and knelt on the cold stone slabs like he did every evening. "Heavenly Lord of all," he prayed. "Please care for my family and give my children the strength to stand up for thy gospel. Show my children the wonders of thy grace and the gift of thy son. Make me a model of Christ. Amen."

The sun set outside Bedford Gaol, and the tiny crosses disappeared from the cell walls.

Two weeks later, the prisoner was happy to hear the jailer announce that Mr. Owen had returned. Bunyan was seated at his desk writing letters when the door scraped open.

"Mr. Owen, it is a pleasure to see you again," he said, rising.

The visitor had a glint of excitement in his eyes. "You are looking well, Mr. Bunyan, considering your circumstances. And I bring good news about those circumstances."

"Yes?"

"I've personally spoken with Thomas Barlow."

"The Bishop of London?"

Owen nodded his head vigorously. "Yes, he was my mentor years ago. He has agreed to release you on bond!"

Bunyan's face fell. "Oh, but I don't have the money to post bond. I'm sorry to have troubled you, Mr. Owen."

The visitor held up an impatient hand. "But I do. I talked to some friends and we were able to put the money together. Your release order should arrive in just a few days."

Bunyan shook his friend's hand heartily. "How can I thank you?"

"We are content to see a non-conformist colleague back in the pulpit. Besides, it keeps me from spending the money on another pair of boots, right?" He laughed. "And—," he handed him the stack of pages, "I have returned your book."

Bunyan set the papers on his desk. "What did you think?"

"Fascinating!" said Owen. "The battle with Apollyon was obviously inspired by your military training. You paint clear pictures of Scripture truths. And such interesting characters! Mr. Wordly-wiseman, Mr. Money-love, Talkative. You have a gift for storytelling."

"You are kind to say so," said Bunyan.

Owen tapped the manuscript with a finger. "I hope you will send this to your publisher right away."

Bunyan shook his head. "I'm afraid my publisher has already endangered himself by printing my previous books. This may have to wait until there is less pressure from the government."

"No, no," Owen insisted. "To delay is to deny our generation of Christians a great encouragement in their struggle to be faithful. This book is going to make you famous, Bunyan. Would you allow me to take it to my publisher, Nathaniel Ponder? I am certain he will be interested in printing it right away."

Bunyan shook his hand again. "You show me a second great kindness. Thank you."

"Hold fast to the gospel, Mr. Bunyan. We have a lot of work to do before we arrive in the celestial city." He tipped his hat with a flourish and turned to the door.

"Amen!" agreed Bunyan.

As Owen had promised, the soon-to-be-famous preacher was released by the end of the month. Gratefully, he returned to his family and his pulpit in Bedford.

Bunyan's benefactor, John Owen, served as a non-conformist minister in London until his death in 1683. He wrote so many books that his works are now published as a sixteen-volume set. He is considered one of the most influential theologians of the seventeenth century.

Bunyan continued to write after his release from prison, and traveled throughout England preaching to crowds as large as four thousand. He wrote dozens of books, but the most popular by far was The Pilgrim's Progress, *first printed by Owen's publisher in 1678. Now a classic of English literature, it has been translated into two hundred languages and has inspired many other books and works of art.*

In August 1688, Bunyan caught pneumonia on a trip to London to reconcile two members of his congregation. He died ten days later and was buried in a non-conformist cemetery. He was outlived by his second wife, Elizabeth, and his sons, Thomas and Joseph.

JOHN ELIOT: APOSTLE TO THE INDIANS

JUNE 26, 1675. THE INDIAN "PRAYING TOWN" OF NATICK, MASSACHUSETTS.

NATICK WAS A new settlement on the Massachusetts frontier. A wooden footbridge over the eighty-foot-wide river connected the clusters of buildings on either side. The fort, the storage hall, the schoolhouse, and the saw mill were all new. The meeting house was one of the biggest in the area. Barns and wooden fences kept the pigs from getting into the fields of maize, beans, and squash on the south bank of the river.

Over one hundred people called the town their home. They spoke English. They raised English cattle. They imported spinning wheels from England and wore their English clothing proudly.

But these were not English settlers. They were Algonquians, natives of the Massachusetts Bay. A few had wooden houses, but most lived in wigwams along the riverbanks. They preferred the strong woven construction of poles and animal skins. Heated by a fire in the winter, and vented in the summer, the wigwams could be packed up and transported easily.

On a mild summer day, a middle-aged Englishman pushed his horse past the drifting smoke of cooking fires and over the footbridge. "Where is John Eliot?" he shouted to two men hauling firewood.

They set down their load and waved. "Hello, Daniel Gookin," said one. "Come have a drink?"

He shook his head impatiently. "No, William, I am sorry. This is urgent. Where is Mr. Eliot?"

The Indian pointed toward the wood-frame schoolhouse.

Daniel left his horse to graze along the road and ran up the path to the school.

Inside the single room, a dozen black-haired children in cotton dresses and buckled knee breeches sat in a row of benches. Their teacher was an Englishman, thin and slightly stooped from his seventy years, but still strong and keen eyed. He stood at the front reading the Bible to them in their native Algonquian language.

"John chapter one, verse one," he announced. "Weske kutchissik wuttinnoowaonk ohtop, kah kuttoowonk ooweetódtamun Manit, ne kuttooonk Manitroooomoo."

He was interrupted by the door banging open.

"John!"

"Daniel? It is not your turn to teach in Natick until next week."

The visitor saw the children looking up at him with surprise in their dark eyes. He crossed the room to the old man and lowered his voice. "Sachem Philip has attacked. The Wampanoags have raided Swansea."

John shut his eyes in dismay, then turned back to his students. "You are dismissed for today," he said. "Go on now!"

They giggled at their early release and scampered out the door.

"I'm sorry for interrupting your class," Daniel said when they were gone. "But I thought you should know immediately. The Indians of Natick and the other praying towns may be in danger."

"Tell me everything you know."

Daniel paced the schoolroom. "The man who told me about the attack said the smoke was so thick it blocked the sun. The Wampanoag warriors burned down the whole town. They killed all the settlers and displayed their bodies on the road like trophies!"

"Retaliation," said John bitterly. "We heard Philip was stockpiling weapons after the execution of the three Wampanoags."

"Their hangings were just. They murdered John Sassamon at Assawampsett Pond!"

"Yes, and we know Philip ordered the murder. He's been suspicious of Sassamon's loyalties ever since Sassamon became a Christian."

"And now he's murdered all the settlers in Swansea." Daniel mopped his brow with his sleeve. "We warned those who lived too far from the forts to move back to more secure areas in case he attacked. But they didn't want to give up their property."

John was quiet. "They underestimated Philip's brutality."

"Well, everyone is panicking. I'm afraid they may strike out against the praying Indians."

"First things first, Daniel. We must pray." John got down on his knees, and Daniel immediately kneeled beside him.

"Gracious and sovereign God," John prayed, "Thou hast done so much for thy people in this new world. Thou hast granted the land for fourteen praying towns and the money to print Bibles and other books in the Algonquian language. Thou hast supplied leaders among the Indians who teach thy ways to them. Thou hast brought the Reformation to a new people. We thank thee for all these things, and we know they have not been in vain. Please protect our people. In the holy name of Christ, Amen."

"Amen," said Daniel, rising. "Someone will speak up for the Christian Indians. The English Corporation for the Propagation of the Gospel Among the Indians wouldn't have funded our labors if they didn't believe in our mission. Surely others do as well."

"God safely brought William Bradford across the Atlantic to this new land. We must not be like the Israelites and ask whether he led us into the wilderness to die."

"I do not think we can reason with Philip. He has rejected the treaty his father made with Bradford. His mind has been set on war for some time."

John sighed, and picked up his English Bible and a wide-brimmed hat from the front bench. "I have preached the gospel to Philip many times, but he is stubborn. Once he tore a button from my coat and declared that he cared no more for my religion than the button on my coat."

"We need to alert the other praying towns," said Daniel. "The elders need to tell their people not to venture out."

"You're right," John agreed. "It isn't safe. We need to talk with John Waban right away, but he is at Punkapoag today." He shut the schoolhouse door firmly behind them.

"I'll go for him," said Daniel, heading up the path to his horse. "I can be there in a few hours."

He disappeared down the road in a cloud of dust.

By the next day, Daniel had returned with John Waban, one of the Natick elders. John and Waban's oldest son Thomas joined them near the elder's wigwam. The four men sat on stools around the fire and passed a plate of raw oysters.

"The praying Indians will not join Philip's war. Why would the Englishmen want to harm us?" demanded Waban.

John wasn't sure how old Waban was, but he suspected that compared to the Indian, he was just a youngster. Waban's dark face was as leathery as the leggings he wore. But his eyes blazed with confidence, and his hair was still coal-black and cut short, falling just to the collar of his fine English coat.

"The English won't come to the praying towns and attack you," John promised. "But your hunting parties could be mistaken for raiders. It isn't safe for any of you to leave Natick."

"We must hunt," Thomas objected. "Our livelihood depends on beaver furs and deer skins. We are not just farmers."

John's face was sober. "I urge you to use great caution and wisdom. We do not know how far this situation could go."

"We worship the English God," Waban said. "We dress with English modesty. We brought our people here to the praying towns so the English would not fear us in their midst. We have an agreement with the English government. They protect us. We protect them."

"Yes," insisted Thomas. "You cannot protect us with your law?"

Daniel shook his head. "I am just the magistrate of the praying towns. I do not control the entire Massachusetts General Court." He wiped his fingers on his trousers and put his hand on Thomas's shoulder. "Do you believe all Indians are good?"

"No." Thomas pursed his lips. "Some are drunkards. Some steal. Some lie."

Daniel nodded. "Yes, just like Englishmen. That is what the Christian Bible teaches about why we all need the grace of Christ. As long as we live in this sinful world, we should expect people to commit sin. That includes frightened English farmers."

"Waban, do you remember when we first met?" asked John.

Waban laughed and tossed an oyster shell into the basket at his feet. "You preached the Bible in my wigwam. Very long sermon! You told us white man's God hears Indian prayers. That is why we call you apostle to the Indians."

John grinned. "That was before the Natick mission, before all the praying towns were built. That was when you wore very little clothing and still went to your shamans for healings and exorcisms."

Waban stared at the fire. "Before the English came and I learned of God, evil worked in my heart. I wanted power. I was angry when I first heard the gospel. But after I became greatly sick, I changed my mind. I was ashamed of all my sins and repented." He smiled at John. "Now I am the brother of Christ and the brother of the English."

"And I still rejoice at that!" replied John. "Daniel and I will remind the white men of your people's bonds with us in Christ. But the English are being butchered by other Indians, and they will not know you are Christian if they see you on the road or in the woods. They may strike first in fear or self defense. So please tell your people to be careful and stay as close to town as possible."

"John, we will fight with you," said Thomas, leaning in. "I have been among your people since I was sixteen. I could work with them, help them track their enemies."

"Thank you, Thomas," said John. "I will present your offer to the General Court."

Waban nodded his approval. "I will tell the people to be careful. Together we will pray that no more blood is shed."

John and Daniel went about their business of traveling to all fourteen praying towns in the Massachusetts Bay, preaching and teaching in the schools. They warned the elders to be careful, and led the people in prayer.

But the war with Philip grew worse. Reports came in from all across the bay area of Indians laying waste to English settlements. Families were killed on their front porches. Houses were burned to ashes. Cattle were butchered and left on the roads to be devoured by vultures.

The settlers put together companies of armed men to attack the Wampanoag warriors, but they were not trained in the Indians' battle strategies. The raids continued, and more people died every week.

Now, most English settlers feared the sight of any Indian.

As John and Daniel had predicted, two praying Indians were captured while hunting. The English missionaries negotiated to free them. They had to escort them back to Natick during the night, afraid the colonists would retaliate.

"The situation is only getting worse," John told Waban, arriving at his wigwam to bring news of Abraham Spene's and John Choo's release.

"I do not blame your people for being afraid," replied Waban, shaking his dark head gravely. "They are chased from their homes by Indians. But it is not the praying Indians that wish them harm."

John's lips were set in a hard line. "When people are afraid, they do things they shouldn't. But it is time for the government to step in." He leaned forward, his serious eyes glittering in the dark. "Daniel and I are going to Boston to speak before the General Court about the mistreatment of Christian Indians. You are greatly respected among the English, Waban. Would you be willing to come with me? It might be dangerous."

Waban met his gaze. "When?"

"We will leave in three days."

With a quick nod, the old Indian pulled aside the flap of his wigwam and disappeared inside.

Three days later, John, Daniel, and Waban rode into Boston. This town was considerably larger than the other settlements, with canons on a hill for defense. The roads approaching the town were dirt, but a few short streets in the town center were paved with stones.

Several people on the street tipped their hats to them, until they looked past the English clothing and took alarm at Waban's dark skin. John maneuvered his horse into the lead and they clattered down the streets toward the meeting house.

With its bell tower and glass windows, the meeting house stood out from the other buildings. They tied up their horses at the hitching post in front. Inside, they were seated in the second-floor gallery on smooth wooden benches.

John stood when he was invited to speak. "We are here because the work that we have put into the Indian praying towns is at risk," he began. "The people are frantically attacking other Christians under the banner of justice. The praying Indians need protection."

One of the councilmen spoke up. "Mr. Eliot, you have come before this court repeatedly, pleading for the Indians and claiming their innocence. Do you not see the devastation they have caused across the land?"

"I see devastation from men," insisted John, "but we must not judge all men for the actions of some, whether Indian or English."

Daniel stepped forward. "The praying Indians have not declared war against us. They are our brothers in the faith. As their magistrate, I remind you that it is our Christian duty to protect them."

"Mr. Gookin," said another member of the court, "we know that you are concerned about justice for the Indians. But some important people in Boston want us to take stronger measures. We need to protect our citizens."

"Does that not include us?" interrupted Waban, rising with dignity from the bench. "We also wish to protect our citizens. We will fight with you. You need guides. Our young men know the territory and Philip's methods. "

Daniel nodded. "Thirty years ago, our agreement with the praying Indians included mutual protection," he reminded the court. "Now is the time to see this agreement——."

He was interrupted by the crash of breaking glass. A rock landed at his feet, and he looked up at a hole in the window. Shouting came from the street outside.

The councilmen were all on their feet.

"Mr. Waban," said one of them, "it is not safe for you to be here at the moment. Nor for you, Mr. Eliot and Mr. Gookin. Friends of Indians are not welcome by many at this time."

"I understand their fear," said Waban. "At Natick, we fear as well. We ask that you allow us to prove ourselves."

"We will protect your people," the council agreed. "But we must discuss the appropriate methods. We will let you know of our decision shortly."

They were ushered out a back exit. Daniel and Waban waited

until John brought the horses around. They left Boston immediately and headed west, back toward Natick.

John and Daniel were teaching in Roxbury in October when word reached them of the General Court's decision: "It is ordered that all the Natick Indians be immediately gathered and sent to Deer Island to live. None of the Indians shall presume to leave the island on their own, upon penalty of death. It shall be lawful for the English to destroy those they find attempting to leave, unless they are removed by order of the authorities or under English guard."

"This is how we protect them?" Daniel spat on the ground in anger. "Round them up on an island and threaten to kill them if they leave?"

"We've got to get to Natick as fast as possible and find Waban," John cried, running for his horse. "Let's go!"

By the time they approached the Natick footbridge, the town was in chaos. Soldiers were already marching the Indians out of their homes and down to the river. Each was carrying whatever supplies they had grabbed on their way out. At the water's edge, small waves lapped at three boats being loaded with passengers. The babies were crying. Several of the young men shouted in refusal and were forced at gunpoint to follow the others.

John gazed across the river. The trees on the other side were aflame with red and yellow leaves, preparing to shed for the winter. An island in the middle of the harbor would be a cold place to brave the New England snows.

"There's Thomas!" Daniel shouted.

They galloped down to the bank.

Thomas was helping an old woman and her granddaughter toward the boats. He ran toward John and Daniel when he saw them.

"This is how your court protects us?" he demanded.

"Back to the boat!" shouted a soldier, his hand on his musket.

John dismounted and stepped between them. "Why have they not been given time to gather supplies?" he demanded.

"We have to get them to the island before a mob appears," the soldier said, recognizing the missionaries. "People are not happy with the court's order. They think all the Indians should be executed just to be on the safe side."

"Your people are not happy with the court's order? Neither are mine!" said Waban, with several young men behind him.

"We will send over supplies," the soldier insisted. "But first we have to get the Indians to the island. The longer they stay here, the more they are at risk."

"We'll take it from here," Daniel said.

"I have my orders."

Daniel glared at him. "I am responsible for the law in this town. Make sure the other boats are secure."

"Fine," said the soldier, moving off. "But move quickly."

"I am so sorry," John said to Waban. "I will go to the court again, but in the meantime I can see no other choice for you than to go."

"You must work this out with your government," Waban insisted.

"We will," said Daniel. "On the island, you will at least be safe from the English for now. John and I will gather supplies and bring them out to you."

John raised his hands in blessing. "Fear not, my friends, Christ has redeemed you. He will not forsake you. Shall we pray together before the soldiers come back?"

"Our Father in Heaven, hallowed be thy name," John began.

The Indians repeated it in Algonquian. "Nushun kesukqut; Quttianatamunach koowesuonk..."

When they had finished the prayer, the soldiers herded them onto the last boat. John and Daniel watched as they pushed away from the shore.

"Look at them, Daniel," John said, shoulders slumped. "They're being sent away from their homes with but half an hour's warning. They have left their goods, their food, their Bibles."

"By the time we can get them released, the town will have been pillaged—either by the English or by the warring Indians. All they had will be turned into spoil."

"*If* we can get them released."

They stood on the bank and watched as the community they had built sailed out of view.

A month later, the General Court had not agreed to restore the praying Indians to their settlement. But they did grant permission for John and Daniel to deliver supplies. The two men loaded a boat with blankets, barrels of cornmeal, and sides of pork. With the cold mist collecting on their coats, they rowed out to the island.

Thomas and a few others were waiting for them when they pushed up onto the pebbled beach. "It is John and Daniel!" said Thomas, visibly relieved. His face was thinner than the last time they had seen him. "You brought food?"

"Yes. Help us unload all these barrels."

"My brothers will unload the boat. I take you to my father."

They followed him through the trees and into the camp in a clearing. They were surprised to see so many Indians and so few wigwams. The once cheerful faces of their friends were now filled with gloom and fear. Many kept their distance.

The old man was sitting on the ground with his feet to a meager fire. His fine coat was torn, and a single streak of gray marked his thick black hair.

"John! Daniel!" Waban cried. "You have good news?"

"Hello, my friend," John said, reaching out to shake his hand. "We brought supplies."

Waban dropped his hand. "That is all?"

"We are still petitioning the court," Daniel explained. "But they granted permission for us to visit and bring whatever you need."

"Oh, my friends. Forgive me. I thought you were bringing hope. It is the one thing we need."

"What is your situation here, Waban?"

The old Indian turned away and looked across the camp. Dozens of people squatted around each campfire, thin blankets drawn around them.

"The winter season is upon us, John," he said. "They have emptied all the praying towns, and other Indian settlements, too. All are brought here. We do not have enough wigwams. They are not as good as the ones in Natick. The English promised to send supplies. But few shipments arrive. There are no deer or turkeys on this island to trap. We have five hundred women and children with no food in their stomachs."

He turned back to them, and looked John square in the eye. "The weakest of us are already dying, starving. We buried a child of six yesterday. A few were killed by English when they left the island to find food. Others have been tried as conspirators with Philip."

John passed a hand over his eyes. "Waban, I am sorry!"

"That is not all," continued Waban, his voice choked with sorrow. "They have taken some as slaves."

"Slaves!" By now, Daniel's face had turned purple.

"Yes, Daniel. Sometimes English boats come over. But they bring no supplies. Instead, they take Indians to sell as slaves on the big ships. We do not have the means to stop them. They can shoot us all here like rabbits in a trap."

"When and how often?" Daniel demanded.

"Almost every trip recently," Thomas jumped in angrily. "They accuse us of plotting against them and then take us from the island. They will not let us prove ourselves!"

John and Daniel stared at each other, angry at their helplessness.

"We have also received death threats for petitioning the court on your behalf," Daniel said. "I have found several threats posted to the door of my house."

"Many claim the name of Christ, but their actions do not prove it," said John sadly.

"Waban, we will keep doing anything we can to convince the court of your release," Daniel promised. "And until then, we will bring as many supplies as we can buy."

"It is hard to have faith in the face of such despair," John said, putting a hand on Waban's shoulder. "But it is still true that God rules over all and brings his will to pass for his glory. We cannot fail to trust his mighty hand. One day, all things will be clear to us."

"Though I am tempted to lose my faith, I still believe," said Waban. "I try to remind the others to believe, too, but I am not the preacher you are."

"Would they come together for a prayer meeting now?"

"Some will," said Waban. "Others are angry at the white man's God and will no longer pray. But if you stay for a few hours, I will try to bring them together."

John and Daniel helped Thomas distribute the supplies while Waban spoke to the other elders. After everyone in the camp had eaten, many were willing to listen as John led them in prayer and read the Bible to them.

Darkness and fog were settling over the harbor when John and Daniel set out for the mainland again. In the twilight, land and sea merged into a shapeless blue horizon. They had barely left the island and their hands were already growing numb from the cold.

"What is that?" said John, peering into the fog. Something large loomed off starboard. He could hear the shift in the waves slapping against the boat.

"It's another boat, heading to Deer Island, I think," Daniel whispered back.

"At this time of night? Can you see how many are on board?"

"Not many," said Daniel, straining to get a good look. "And the boat is riding high on the water. It must not be loaded down with supplies."

"They're slavers!" hissed John. "We can't let them take more Indians tonight. We have to do something."

"Like what?" Daniel said, trying to keep his voice down. He knew the sound carried easily across the water. "We can't shoot them."

"I have an idea. Turn this boat around and see if we can catch up to them."

"What are you planning?"

"We're going to ram their boat."

"What? If we don't kill ourselves, we'll get arrested!"

"Would you rather watch more of our converts kidnapped into slavery?"

"All right, turn this boat!"

They rowed furiously and began to overtake the other boat. It grew larger as they approached.

"Ho there!" came a shout from ahead. "Do you not see us?"

"Is someone out there?" John shouted.

"Right here! Right in front of you!" was the reply. "Turn away! You're going to ram us!"

John aimed straight for them. With a crunch, the collision threw John and Daniel into the icy water. Gasping, they grabbed on to their capsized boat.

"Fools!" shouted the captain of the other boat. "Pull them in before they freeze to death."

Arms reached down and hauled them by their coats into the larger boat. They lay in the bottom, seawater pooling around them.

"I'm sorry, Captain," John stammered between chattering teeth. "Did I damage your rig?"

"We're taking on some water, Captain," said one of the men, inspecting the side of the boat. "But we can make it back to shore if we turn around now."

The captain thrust his face into John's. "You rammed us on purpose!"

John shrugged and emptied the water from his boots. "The fog is thick and I'm an old man."

They looked at Daniel. "I was simply following orders," he objected.

"Look here," John asserted. "I'm a missionary, not a mercenary."

"I recognize you now," said the captain. "You're John Eliot."

"He's an Indian lover!" shouted one of the men.

The captain shoved his crewman back. "I am the only one who makes accusations on this boat."

"The governor himself commissioned me to bring the gospel to the Indians," said John. He squinted at them in the fog. "Are you men against taking the gospel to heathens?"

They could hear the trickle of water as the sea leaked into the crinkled stern.

The captain gave a nervous chuckle. "We're all Christian men," he insisted. "Just on our way to check on the Indians we were."

"Uh-huh," said Daniel, crossing his arms over his chest and glaring at them.

"Very well," John continued calmly. "Then accept my apology and we'll ride with you back to Boston. I will pay for the damages to your boat, of course."

"Turn her around," the captain ordered his crew. "With two extra people on board, we don't have much room anyway. We'll have to wait for repairs before we can come back to, er, check on the Indians."

"Perhaps by then this war will be over and we can all go back to being civilized persons," John muttered.

Daniel scooted next to John and bent toward his ear. "We stopped *these* slavers, but we're out of boats to ram into the others!" he whispered.

The next day, John went straight back to his home in Roxbury to appeal to the governor.

You must protect the Indians from the slaving, he wrote. *To sell souls for money is a dangerous merchandise. I hope that the honored council will pardon my boldness and consider what God has to say about these decisions.*

Despite his letters and appearances before the court, the condition of the praying Indians did not change. They continued to die and be captured into slavery. John and Daniel crossed to the island as often as they could, bringing supplies and writing letters back to the governor about the suffering of their friends. They prayed day and night that God would move the court to uphold their previous agreement.

And then, finally, the day came when the English declared that they needed help finding and fighting their enemies. They asked the praying Indians to join them in battle.

Thomas immediately volunteered. He took off his English shoes, put on his leather moccasins, and gathered his weapons. Eighty Indian men joined the English ranks to defend the settlements against Sachem Philip.

Over the next few months, the praying Indians showed the soldiers how to track the Wampanoag warriors. They taught them how to sneak up on them in the woods. Their assistance in battle earned the respect of the English captains who proudly fought by their sides. Sachem Philip was killed. The war was over.

John and Daniel gathered the testimonies of the English captains and presented them to the General Court. With evidence of their loyalty in hand, the court agreed to set the praying Indians free from Deer Island and restore them to their towns.

The two missionaries chartered boats to gather all their friends from the island and sail back down the river.

"There's Natick!" they all shouted as they approached. But they were dismayed to discover only the remains of their village.

The footbridge had been burned. Wigwams were missing. Fences had been torn down, and the cattle and hogs were gone. Philip's war had ravaged their home.

John and Daniel were at Waban's side as he surveyed the damage. "It will never be like it was," said the old Indian, hanging his head low.

"We will help you rebuild," Daniel promised. "We'll start by cleaning up the wigwams and constructing new ones. Then we'll start clearing the fields and planting crops."

"Yes," John agreed. "And we will raise money from the English Corporation to purchase new hoes and axes and spinning wheels."

But Waban still sighed. "So many died on that island. And some now return to their tribes, forsaking the English and their God. We will have to rebuild with a small number."

"That number will grow again as it did in the past," John said. "Daniel and I will not give up on the Lord's work of bringing the gospel to the Indians."

"And we will continue to speak up for your people," said Daniel, pulling a notebook from his pocket. "English Christians must have an accurate record of the losses their Indian brothers endured here."

He showed them the front page of his notebook. In English, he had written: *History of the Christian Indians: A True and Impartial Narrative of the Doings and Sufferings of the Christian or Praying Indians.*

"Perhaps with an honest record, we can keep this from happening again," he said.

Waban took a step away and turned to face them. "Daniel, I remember you telling me that Englishmen are sinners and Indians are sinners. As long as we are in this sinful world, we should expect men to commit sins against their brothers."

"It is true," Daniel said sadly.

"But that is why we must continue to spread the gospel of God's grace in Christ," said John. "The work of his spirit in the souls of men is greater than sin. We find our hope in that."

Waban took a deep breath and nodded at them. "I believe those words," he said. "And I will keep telling my brothers to believe them, too."

"Shall we get to work?" said John. He tucked his Algonquian Bible into his pocket and headed toward the wigwams.

With the help of the praying Indians, Philip's War was won by the colonists. After the war, only four of the fourteen praying towns were rebuilt. When John Waban died in 1684, his son Thomas took over as leader of the praying Indians. Daniel Gookin was appointed major general of the Massachusetts Bay Colony and died in 1687. John Eliot continued as an itinerant preacher to the Indians until he died on May 20, 1690. He was buried in the parish tomb in Roxbury, Massachusetts.

Eliot's translation of the Bible into Algonquian was the first written document in that language, and the first Bible printed in what would become the United States. His mission to the Indians prior to the war became a model for evangelical missions around the world in the next century, especially the work of William Carey.

⊕THER REFⓞRⓜATIⓞN CHRISTIANS

THE CHARACTERS IN this book are not the only significant Christians of the Reformation period. Below is a brief look at just a few of the others.

Argula von Grumbach was a well-educated woman born before 1490 and active in the German Reformation. She was a member of the court under Duchess Kunigunde and a friend of Martin Luther. When the city of Ingolstadt forced a student to recant his Lutheran ideas under penalty of death, she published a pamphlet addressed to the rector of the university in protest. She published other pamphlets in support of the Reformation. No one would respond to her because of her high social status and because they disapproved of women theologians. Instead, they removed her husband, Friedrich von Grumbach of Franconia, from his post in the city. Though he was not Protestant, he supported her efforts. She remained friends with Luther and the other reformers.

Philipp Melanchthon was a German reformer and the dear friend and successor to Martin Luther. After earning his

Master of Arts degree at the age of sixteen from the University of Tübingen, he took his language skills and found his way into Erasmus's circle. In 1518, he was a professor at the University of Wittenberg, where he became friends with Luther. He wrote many books. Both Protestants and Catholics liked him, and he looked for opportunities to unite them. At times, his willingness to compromise led to severe criticism from other Protestants. But his ability to dialogue with others helped reign in Luther's sharp tongue. After Luther's death, Melanchthon led the Lutheran cause.

Anne Askew was an English noblewoman with ties to Archbishop Thomas Cranmer and Queen Katherine Parr. In her day, reformed doctrines were still considered treason in England. Her dedication to the Reformation led to her arrest and severe torture in the summer of 1546, supervised by Lord Chancellor Wriothesley. Though she suffered broken bones and other physical torments, she never gave up the names of her fellow reformers or accepted Catholic communion. She was burned at the stake in July 1546.

Queen Elizabeth I, born in 1533, had a remarkably long and successful reign in England. The daughter of Henry VIII and Anne Boleyn, Elizabeth was not the boy that Henry's court astrologers predicted. Henry was so disappointed he sent her away from the court until Queen Katherine Parr convinced him to bring her back. After Henry's death, Elizabeth's half-brother Edward VI became king, and he made further reforms to the Church of England that his father would not. But he died young, and his sister Mary I took the throne, restoring the authority of the pope and bringing Catholic bishops back into England. Elizabeth finally became queen in 1558 when Mary's five year reign ended with her illness and death. During Elizabeth's reign, England returned to Protestantism, prayers started to be said in English instead of Latin, and the *Book of Common Prayer* was restored. She encouraged moderation and was not the radical reformer the Puritans had hoped for, but her long reign did bring some stability back to the English people.

Katherine Schutz Zell lost her two children at a young age. After their deaths, she dedicated herself to serving the church formally. She wrote a book of psalms for women, visited prisoners, led funerals, and assisted her husband Matthew, a pastor in Strasbourg. She also risked her life helping exiled Christians (such as Martin Bucer) by hiding them in her home. She was known for being very outspoken for the Reformed faith. She died in 1562.

Theodore Beza was a French lawyer who took over Calvin's work in Geneva after Calvin's death in May 1564. He had moved to Geneva in 1548 and become a professor of Greek at the academy in Lausanne. He held several significant roles in the French Reformation, including advisor to Queen Jeanne of Navarre, and mediator between the Huguenots and Catherine de Medici at the Colloquy of Poissy. A skilled speaker, scholar, and theologian, he published his Greek New Testament in 1565. Beza's theology had a strong influence on Reformed Calvinists in the seventeenth century. He died in October 1605.

George Fox, born in 1624 to a cloth weaver and his wife, was the founder of The Society of Friends, also known as the Quakers. His followers were named "Quaker" by their enemies, who made fun of the way they shook or quaked in worship. After experiencing what he called a vision, Fox's beliefs changed dramatically, mixing the theology of the Puritans and Anabaptists. He considered himself a Christian, but since he rejected the Trinity, many Christians were not convinced he was a true believer. His followers rejected creeds and confessions as human words. They emphasize simplicity in life, democracy in the church, a revelation by "inner light," and pacifism (a refusal to participate in the military). Today many Quakers have modified their beliefs and are more accepted among modern Evangelicals.

Thomas Watson, a seventeenth-century English Puritan, wrote many classic books that are still in print today, including *Heaven Taken by Storm*. Earning his Master of Arts from Emmanuel College, Cambridge, he went on to be a pastor at St. Stephen's Walkbrook in London. His support for the restoration of King Charles II to the throne led to his imprisonment. Later he was released and reinstated at St. Stephen's. After the Act of Uniformity was passed in 1662, which required the use of the *Book of Common Prayer*, he was one of thousands of ministers who refused to comply.

Richard Baxter, an English pastor in Kidderminster, was a highly influential Puritan. Known for his practical applications of theology, Baxter was ordained in the Church of England and sought dialogue between Presbyterians, Congregationalists, and Anglicans. Concerned about unity, he was not eager to separate from the established church, but he eventually took a non-conformist stand. A prolific writer, his theological creativity was sometimes questioned by other Puritans. His most famous book is a guide for pastors called *Christian Directory*. He died in 1707.

ENLIGHTENMENT AND AWAKENING

AT THE CLOSE of the seventeenth century, the world was entering a new era of thinking known as the *Age of Enlightenment*. The roots of Enlightenment thinking go back a half century. The wars of religion during the Reformation caused so much death and violation of conscience. In reaction to those events, Enlightenment thinkers feared that imposing religion upon others would lead only to more bloodshed. So they sought to emphasize reason or logical thought over religion.

One of the thinkers who had a big influence on the Enlightenment was a Dutch Jewish philosopher named Benedict de Spinoza (1632-1677). Based on his writings, a concept called *Deism* became popular. This term comes from the Latin word for God.

Deists claimed that Scripture is not inspired by God, but should be treated like any other human book. The reformers taught that Scripture is perfect and that the person who studies Scripture must be moved by the Holy Spirit to understand it. Deists rejected this. They said it was putting some people higher than others if only

Christians could understand the Bible. They emphasized reason and nature available to all people, not just Christians—as the source of knowledge. They believed in the existence of God, but rejected the idea that the Bible was the highest authority for humanity.

Since deists rejected the Bible, they also denied certain teachings of the Bible, like the Trinity (God as Father, Son, and Spirit), the incarnation of Christ (Jesus coming to earth as a human), the atonement (Jesus paying for sin by his death on the cross), and the existence of miracles (God intervening in the laws of nature he created). Deism reached its peak in the eighteenth century.

At creation, God set everything in motion according to the laws of nature. So Enlightenment thinkers believed that we could learn everything we need to know about God from nature. From nature we can learn that God is beautiful and good. From nature we can learn that people have the right to life and liberty and the pursuit of happiness. Christians agree that we can learn this from nature, but that only Scripture tells us about salvation through Jesus.

Many Enlightenment thinkers were deists, though some, such as John Locke, identified themselves with Christianity. A mixture of Scripture and Enlightenment thinking played an important role in the founding of the United States.

But Deists were not the only prominent thinkers at this time. A group, known as *Evangelicals*, began to emerge at the close of the Reformation. Other Christians had called themselves "evangelical" prior to the eighteenth century, but this was different. Building on their Reformation past, these Evangelicals emphasized the active spread of the gospel through missions and evangelism. John Eliot's mission to Native Americans set an example for these efforts.

Evangelical calls for true conversion would result in an explosion of revivals around the world. The decades of these worldwide revivals would become known as the *First* and *Second Great Awakenings*. The Reformation had set the stage for the work of some of Christianity's most famous missionaries.

Author Information

Mindy and Brandon Withrow live in Philadelphia, Pennsylvania. Brandon is a PhD Candidate in Historical Theology at Wesminster Theological Seminary, where Mindy directs the seminary's marketing communications. Both are graduates of the Moody Bible Institute in Chicago; Brandon is also a graduate of Trinity Evangelical Divinity School. They are both writers and active bloggers. One of their favorite activities is reading to their nieces and nephews.

WHERE WE GOT OUR INFORMATION
AND OTHER HELPFUL RESOURCES

Atkinson, James. *The Trial of Luther.* Stein and Day, 1971.

Augustijn, Cornelis. *Erasmus: His Life, Works, and Influence.* Translated by J.C. Grayson. University of Toronto Press, 1991.

Bainton, Roland H. *Women of the Reformation in France and England.* Augsburg, 1973.

Baird, Henry M. *History of the Rise of the Huguenots of France.* Vol 2. AMS Press, 1970.

Bentley-Taylor, David. *My Dear Erasmus: The Forgotten Reformer.* Christian Focus Publications, 2002.

Bowden, John, ed. *Encyclopedia of Christianity.* Oxford Press, 2005.

Bryson, David. *Queen Jeanne and the Promised Land: Dynasty, Homeland, Religion and Violence in Sixteenth-Century France.* Brill, 1999.

Bunyan, John. *The Complete Works of John Bunyan.* Bradley, Garretson and Co., 1872.

Caffrey, Kate. *The Mayflower.* Stein and Day, 1974.

Coffey, John. *Politics, Religion and the British Revolutions: The Mind of Samuel Rutherford.* Cambridge Press, 1997.

Cogley, Richard W. *John Eliot's Mission to the Indians before King Philip's War.* Harvard University Press, 1999.

Cottret, Bernard. *Calvin: A Biography.* Translated by M. Wallace McDonald. Eerdmans, 2000.

Cross, F.L., ed. *The Oxford Dictionary of the Christian Church.* Oxford, 2005.

Elwell, Walter A., ed. *Evangelical Dictionary of Theology.* Baker Book House, 1984.

Foxe, John. *The Acts and Monuments of John Foxe.* 8 Vols. AMS Press Inc., 1965.

George, Timothy. *Theology of the Reformers*. Broadman and Holman, 1988.

Gilmour, Robert. *Samuel Rutherford: A Study*. Oliphant Anderson and Ferrier, 1904.

Greaves, Richard L. *Glimpses of Glory: John Bunyan and English Dissent*. Stanford University Press, 2002.

Hillerbrand, Hans J. *Erasmus and His Age: Selected Letters of Desiderius Erasmus*. Harper Torchbooks, 1970.

Hillerbrand, Hans J., ed. *The Oxford Encyclopedia of the Reformation*. 4 Vols. Oxford, 1996.

Holt, Mack P. *The French Wars of Religion, 1562-1629*. Cambridge, 1995.

Kittelson, James M. *Luther the Reformer: The Story of the Man and His Career*. Augsburg, 1986.

Larsen, Timothy, ed. *Biographical Dictionary of Evangelicals*. Intervarsity Press, 2003.

Lepore, Jill. *The Name of War: King Philip's War and the Origins of American Identity*. Alfred A. Knopf, 1999.

Lindsay, Thomas. *Martin Luther: The Man who Started the Reformation*. Christian Focus Publications, 1996.

MacCulloch, Diarmaid. *Thomas Cranmer*. Yale University Press, 1996.

Mynors, R.A.B., and Peter G. Bietenholz. *The Correspondence of Erasmus*. Vol. 8. University of Toronto Press, 1988.

Peterson, Susan Lynn. *Timeline Charts of the Western Church*. Zondervan, 1999.

Reid, W. Stanford. *Trumpeter of God: A Biography of John Knox*. Charles Scribner's Sons, 1974.

Schmidt, Gary D. *William Bradford: Plymouth's Faithful Pilgrim*. Eerdmans, 1999.

Strayer, James M. *Anabaptists and the Sword*. Coronado Press, 1972.

Todd, John M. *Luther: A Life*. Crossroad, 1982.

Weir, Alison. *The Six Wives of Henry VIII*. Grove Press, 1991.

Winslow, Ola Elizabeth. *John Eliot: Apostle to the Indians*. Houghton Mifflin, 1968.

Zahl, Paul F.M. *Five Women of the English Reformation*. Eerdmans, 2001.

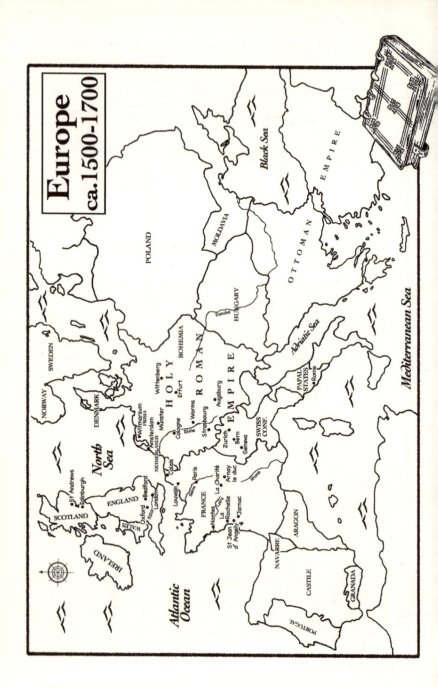

Europe
ca.1500-1700

SWEDEN

NORWAY

DENMARK

POLAND

MOLDAVIA

Black Sea

OTTOMAN

EMPIRE

North
Sea

HOLY

ROMAN

EMPIRE

BOHEMIA

HUNGARY

Danube

Adriatic Sea

Witfmarsum
FRISIA
Amsterdam
NETHERLANDS

Wittenberg

Erfurt

Worms
Cologne
Rhine
Strasbourg
Zurich
Bern
Geneva
SWISS
CONF.

Münster

Augsburg

PAPAL
STATES
Rome

Rhone

Mediterranean Sea

St Andrews
Edinburgh
Bedford
Oxford
London
SCOTLAND
ENGLAND
WALES

Louvain
Calais
Seine
Paris
La Charité
Arnay
le duc
FRANCE
Nantes
La
St Jean Rochelle
d'Angely Jarnac

IRELAND

ARAGON

NAVARRE

CASTILE

GRANADA

PORTUGAL

Atlantic
Ocean

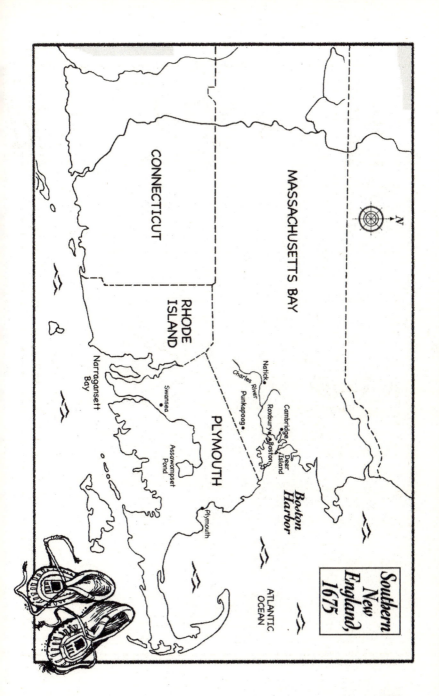

Southern
New
England,
1675

CONNECTICUT

MASSACHUSETTS BAY

RHODE
ISLAND

PLYMOUTH

Narragansett
Bay

Swansea

Assawompset
Pond

Natick

Charles River

Punkapoag

Roxbury
Cambridge
Boston

Deer
Island

Boston
Harbor

Plymouth

ATLANTIC
OCEAN

N

CHRISTIAN FOCUS PUBLICATIONS

Christian Focus | Christian Heritage | CF4K | Mentor

Christian Focus Publications publishes books for adults and children under its four main imprints: Christian Focus, Christian Heritage, CF4K and Mentor. Our books reflect that God's word is reliable and Jesus is the way to know him, and live for ever with him.

Our children's publication list includes a Sunday school curriculum that covers pre-school to early teens; puzzle and activity books. We also publish personal and family devotional titles, biographies and inspirational stories that children will love.

If you are looking for quality Bible teaching for children then we have an excellent range of Bible story and age specific theological books. From pre-school to teenage fiction, we have it covered!

Find us at our web page:
www.christianfocus.com

CF4·K
Because you're never too young to know Jesus